FIFTH EDITION

Study Guide
to Accompany Kalat's
Biological Psychology

ELAINE M. HULL
State University of New York at Buffalo

Brooks/Cole Publishing Company

I(T)P An International Thomson Publishing Company
_____

Pacific Grove • Albany • Bonn • Boston • Cincinnati • Detroit • London • Madrid • Melbourne
Mexico City • New York • Paris • San Francisco • Singapore • Tokyo • Toronto • Washington

Sponsoring Editor: Faith B. Stoddard
Editorial Assistant: Patsy Vienneau
Production Coordinator: Dorothy Bell
Cover Design: Roy R. Neuhaus
Cover Illustration: Jeena Keller
Printing and Binding: Malloy Lithographing, Inc.

For more information, contact:

BROOKS/COLE PUBLISHING CO.
511 Forest Lodge Rd.
Pacific Grove, CA 93950
USA

International Thomson Publishing
Berkshire House 168-173
High Holborn
London WC1V 7AA
England

Thomas Nelson Australia
102 Dodds Street
South Melbourne, 3205
Victoria, Australia

Nelson Canada
1120 Birchmount Road
Scarborough, Ontario
Canada M1K 5G4

International Thomson Editores
Campos Eliseos 385, Piso 7
Col. Polanco
11560 México D. F. México

International Thomson Publishing GmbH
Königwinterer Strasse 418
53227 Bonn
Germany

International Thomson Publishing Asia
221 Henderson Road
#05–10 Henderson Building
Singapore 0315

International Thomson Publishing–Japan
Hirakawacho Kyowa Building, 3F
2-2-1 Hirakawacho
Chiyoda-ku, 102 Tokyo
Japan

Printed in the United States of America

10 9 8 7 6 5 4 3 2 1

ISBN 0-534-21110-0

PREFACE

When a book is as well written as Kalat's *Biological Psychology*, everything fits together logically and "makes sense;" it is easy to acquire a feeling of understanding. However, the sense of security produced by passive understanding is frequently shattered by an exam that requires recall and active reconstruction of the material. One of the earliest psychological principles of learning is that recognition is easier than recall and that passively following an argument is easier than actively reconstructing it. Unfortunately, passively understood material does not become part of us in the same way that actively manipulated material does.

The role of this study guide is to stimulate your active assimilation of the material in Kalat's textbook. Each chapter of the text has its own introductory and concluding summaries and a number of review and discussion questions. Thus the initial reading and review of each chapter is directed by the text itself. The study guide is designed for more comprehensive, indepth review. The introduction provides a brief review of each chapter to refresh your memory at the beginning of a study session. Key Terms and Concepts provide a quick overview of the material in outline form. Make sure that each term is familiar, and note its relationship to the overall structure of the chapter. Short-Answer Questions are designed to help you organize information pertinent to specific problems. These questions are listed under headings that refer to the main divisions of the chapter. If you have difficulty answering a question fully, refer to the appropriate section of the text to find the answer. The Multiple-Choice Questions check your knowledge of detail and emphasize points that are easy to get confused. Some may seem picky, but it is better to encounter the confusing detail here rather than on an exam. Answers are listed at the end of the section. A number of chapters have graphics to be labeled or to be used in answering accompanying questions. Each graphic is adapted from or taken directly from the text; you can refer to the appropriate drawing in the text if you have difficulty labeling it.

Biological psychology is full of detailed experimental knowledge and also of contradictions and perplexities. It also has important general concepts and broad philosophical implications. The concepts and generalizations are hollow without an interesting conceptual framework and some detailed knowledge.

A student once asked how anyone could stand to teach a course in which so much is unknown. However, this is a problem only if you expect the body to work in a simple, stereotyped way. Fortunately, there is considerable orderliness about the body, and equally fortunately, there is a great deal of adaptability that gives rise to unresolved questions and apparent conflicts. The study of brain and behavior may well be the most exciting frontier of knowledge. In contrast to the consternation of the student who wanted knowledge handed out in tidy packets, many others have found that their biological psychology course did more to challenge and enrich their basic philosophy of life than did any other course. I hope that this text and study guide will help make your experiences with biological psychology more like those of the latter students than like those of the former.

Thanks to Jim Brace-Thompson, the Psychology Editor for Brooks/Cole Publishing Company, to James Kalat, author of *Biological Psychology*, and to Faith Stoddard, Acquisitions Editor for the Study Guide.

Elaine M. Hull

CONTENTS

1

THE GLOBAL ISSUES OF BIOLOGICAL PSYCHOLOGY

INTRODUCTION

Biological psychology is the study of the physiological, ontogenetic (developmental), evolutionary, and functional explanations of behavior. Bird song provides an example of the four types of explanation. Increased testosterone levels during mating season cause two brain areas that are important for singing to increase in size, providing a physiological mechanism for singing. Ontogenetic explanations focus on embryology and on experience during a sensitive period, when the bird forms a template of the appropriate species-typical song. Evolutionary explanations discuss the selection of traits, including the neural substrates of behavior, in terms of their adaptive value to the organism. If an organism is better able to reproduce because of a certain trait, that trait will be passed on to its offspring, whose reproduction will in turn be facilitated. Over successive generations the trait will spread throughout the population. Functional explanations describe the advantages conferred by each trait. For example, a male bird's song attracts a female and primes her to engage in reproductive behaviors; it also deters competition from other males.

Human behavior is also subject to biological explanation. Some biological factors force a behavior to occur, as when a well-placed tap on the knee causes the leg to jerk upward. Other factors enable a behavior to occur or influence its likelihood of occurrence, as when increased levels of sex hormones increase sexual motivation. Past experiences and current perceptions influence behavior through brain activity.

There are a number of theories about the relationship of the mind to the brain. According to the dualist position, the mind exists independently of the brain. Interactionism, the most popular form of dualism holds that the brain sends messages to the mind, which then exerts some control over the brain. Monism holds that there is only one kind of substance, though various theorists differ as to whether that substance is mental, physical, or some combination of the two. The materialist position (a form of monism) holds that the brain is a machine and that consciousness is irrelevant to its functioning. The identity position (another form of monism) proposes that the mind is the same thing as brain activity but is described in different terms. The emergent property position is a version of the identity position; it holds that consciousness emerges only from certain kinds of brain organization. Biological psychology cannot resolve the issues of the essence and functional significance of the mind or of its relationship to the brain, but it can contribute relevant data. For example, electrical stimulation of the brain can produce sensations, movements, emotions, and complicated patterns of behavior. Thus, physical processes can influence mental ones.

The issue of animal experimentation has become controversial. The usefulness of animal research rests both on the similarity across species of many biological functions and on the difficulty or impossibility of conducting such research on humans. Valuable clinical treatments of human disorders have been gleaned from such experiments. However, even though experimenters attempt to minimize pain, and even though animal care committees oversee the research, a certain amount of distress accompanies much animal experimentation. In this case, as in many other ethical issues, it is difficult to gain resolution of the competing values.

KEY TERMS AND CONCEPTS

1. Biological explanations of behavior
    Physiological explanations
        Testosterone and bird song
            Caudal nucleus of the hyperstriatum ventrale
            Robust nucleus of the archistriatum
            Role of these areas in females
    Ontogenetic explanations
        Sensitive period
        Template
    Evolutionary explanations
        Common ancestor
    Functional explanations
        No need for organism to understand function

2. Biological explanations of human behavior
    Forcing behavior
    Enabling behavior

3. The mind-brain relationship
    Philosophical views of mind and brain
        Dualism
            Interactionism
        Monism
            Materialism
            Identity position
            Emergent property position
    Control of behavior by electrical stimulation of brain
        Movement in dogs
        Complex behavior in chickens

2

Human brain stimulation
　　During surgery for epilepsy
　　Focus
　　For depression or pain

4. Why investigators study animals, and the ethics of animal research
　　Why study animals?
　　　　Similar mechanisms of behavior
　　　　Exaggerated processes
　　　　Curiosity about animals
　　　　Clues to human evolution
　　　　Can't experiment on humans
　　Evolutionary relationships among species
　　　　Evolutionary tree
　　Ethical issues
　　　　Animal research leads to useful discoveries.
　　　　Substantial government regulation
　　　　Minimalists vs abolitionists
　　　　Animal welfare vs. equal rights for animals
　　　　How much pain really is involved in animal research?
　　　　Are alternative methods feasible?
　　　　Difficulty of resolving moral issues

SHORT-ANSWER QUESTIONS

1. *Biological explanations of behavior*
　　a.　What are the four major types of explanation of behavior sought by biological psychologists?

　　b.　Discuss the singing of birds from each of these perspectives.

c.   What is the effect of testosterone on the brain of male
     songbirds? of female songbirds?

d.   What is an ontogenetic explanation?

e.   What is a critical period? a template?

f.   How do we know that female songbirds form templates of their
     species' song?

g.   What are the two functions of the male bird's song?

h. What should we infer about the male's understanding of his behavior?

2. *Bioloical explanations of human behavior*
   a. Explain the difference between biological factors that force a behavior to occur and those that enable it to occur. Give an example of each.

3. *The mind-brain relationship*
   a. What are the two major positions regarding the mind-brain relationship? List the main variants of these major positions, and give a strength and a weakness of each.

   b. With which philosophical position(s) is biological psychology most compatible? With which is it least compatible?

c.   What did Fritsch and Hitzig find when they stimulated the brains of dogs?

d.   What behavior patterns did von Holst and von St. Paul elicit in their chickens?

e.   Why can we stimulate the brain of an awake epileptic at the time of surgery? What effects of this stimulation have been reported?

f.   What did Heath observe when he stimulated the brain of a depressed patient?

4. *The controversy over the ethics of animal research*

    a.   What are five reasons biological psychologists study nonhuman animals?

    b.   What are some of the useful discoveries that have been based on animal research?

    c.   What is the role of Laboratory Animal Care Committees?

    d.   Compare the positions of the "minimalists" and the "abolitionists" with regard to the conduct of animal research.

    e.   How widespread was the incidence of gross abuse of animals found by Coile and Miller?

f.   What is the problem with the development of alternative research methods that do not require animals?

POSTTEST

Multiple-Choice Questions

1. Adult male songbirds
   a. sing frequently throughout the year because of an instinct to sing.
   b. sing when testosterone levels are high enough to increase the size and activity of two brain areas that are critical for singing.
   c. sing because they know that their songs will attract females and deter male competitors.
   d. sing the correct song, even if they have never heard the song.

2. Female songbirds
   a. sing throughout the year, first to attract a male and then to keep their young nearby.
   b. are unable to sing, even when injected with large amounts of testosterone.
   c. form a template of their species' song when they are exposed to it during their sensitive period.
   d. sing a song that is very different from that of the males of their species.

3. A female canary that hears a large number and variety of canary songs
   a. is confused and refuses to mate with any male.
   b. begins to imitate those songs in order to let the nearest male know that she is ready to mate.
   c. becomes aggressive and defends her territory from other females that might invade.
   d. is quicker to respond sexually, quicker to lay eggs, and more likely to lay a large number of eggs.

4. A male's song is more effective if it
    a. is highly characteristic of his species.
    b. can be heard throughout the territories of many males.
    c. is sung throughout the year.
    d. all of the above.

5. The dualist position
    a. is problematic because it does not fit with our commonsense notion of the mind.
    b. proposes that the mind is the same thing as brain activity.
    c. cannot explain how, if the mind is not a type of matter or energy, it could possibly alter the electrical and chemical activities of the brain.
    d. proposes that the mind is just an illusion.

6. The proposition that the brain is a machine and that consiousness is irrelevant to its functioning is characteristic of which position on the mind-brain problem?
    a. materialist
    b. dualist
    c. parallelist
    d. interactionist

7. The identity position
    a. is the only satisfactory position on the mind-brain problem.
    b. is analogous to describing a statue as both a piece of stone and a work of art.
    c. explains easily why we are conscious of some neural activities and not conscious of others.
    d. proposes that the mind is just an illusion.

8. Electrical stimulation of the cortex of an anesthetized dog
    a. resulted in limited, reproducible movements on the side of the body opposite the stimulation.
    b. was done by Fritsch and Hitzig before 1900.
    c. bypassed the preliminary stages of sensory and motor processing.
    d. all of the above.

9. Electrical stimulation of the brains of awake chickens
    a. always elicited aggressive attacks.
    b. resulted in numerous complex behaviors, depending on the location of the electrode, intensity of stimulation, and stimuli in the environment.
    c. was done by Penfield.
    d. paralyzed the chickens for the duration of the stimulation.

10. Electrical stimulation of the brains of awake epileptics
    a. is inherently very painful and is therefore rarely done.
    b. produces movements that can easily be overridden by the person's will not to make them.
    c. has resulted in sensations, motor responses, emotional changes, and feelings that usually precede seizures.
    d. more than one of the above

11. Animal research
    a. yields no useful discoveries.
    b. could be replaced with alternative research methods that do not require the use of live animals.
    c. depends entirely on the wisdom and good intentions of individual researchers for maintaining good care of the animals.
    d. none of the above

12. Animal advocates
    a. are invariably "rabble rousers" with no legitimate point.
    b. are concerned that if we are reluctant to perform experiments on humans, we should be equally concerned about performing experiments on animals.
    c. are united in their demand that all animal experimentation be totally eliminated.
    d. are right in their claim that laboratory animals are frequently grossly abused.

Answers to Multiple-Choice Questions

1. b	5. c	9. b
2. c	6. a	10. c
3. d	7. b	11. d
4. a	8. d	12. b

2

NERVE CELLS AND
NERVE IMPULSES

INTRODUCTION

Neurons, like all animal cells, are bounded by a fatty membrane, which restricts the flow of chemicals into and out of the cell. Animal cells also contain structures, such as a nucleus, ribosomes, mitochondria, lysosomes, and a Golgi complex, that are important for various genetic, synthetic, and metabolic functions. A neuron is composed of (1) dendrites, which receive stimulation from other cells; (2) the soma or cell body, which contains the genetic and metabolic machinery and also conducts stimulation to the axon; and (3) the axon, which carries the nerve impulse to other neurons, frequently across long distances. Neurons may be classified as receptors or sensory neurons, which are highly sensitive to specific external stimuli; motor neurons, which stimulate muscles and glands; and interneurons, which communicate with other neurons. One can infer a great deal about a neuron's function from its shape. For example, a neuron that integrates input from many sources has many branching dendrites. Some small interneurons have axons and dendrites that branch diffusely, but only within a small radius. The nervous system also contains a great many support cells called glia, which provide support functions and participate indirectly with neural communication.

Most of the adult vertebrate brain cannot develop new neurons; however, neurons can change their shapes and connections. Exposure to alcohol produces deficient patterns of dendritic branching. The cell loss that results from aging is compensated by increased dendritic branching in alert old people, but there is decreased branching in the senile.

A blood-brain barrier prevents many substances, including most viruses and bacteria as well as most forms of nutrition, from entering the brain. In most parts of the brain, glucose is the only nutrient that can cross the barrier in significant amounts. Therefore, the brain is highly dependent on glucose and on thiamine, which is needed to metabolize glucose. Fat soluble molecules and small uncharged molecules can cross the barrier freely. The barrier depends on tight junctions between endothelial cells lining capillaries; astrocytes surrounding the endothelial cells somehow strengthen the barrier.

The ability of a neuron to respond quickly to stimulation depends on the resting potential. A metabolically active sodium-potassium pump establishes concentration gradients by transporting sodium (Na^+) ions out of the cell and potassium (K^+) ions into the cell. There is a resultant negative charge inside the cell, because three sodium ions are pumped out for every two potassium ions pumped in. Selective permeability of the membrane increases this potential by allowing potassium ions to flow out, down their concentration gradient; the loss of the positive potassium ions leaves the inside of the neuron even more negative. The relative impermeability of sodium results in minimal inflow of positive ions to offset the potassium outflow. The concentration and electrical gradients exert opposing influences on potassium. The electrical gradient (the negative charge inside the cell) attracts more potassium inside the cell than would be there if the concentration gradient were the only influence. Sodium ions, however, are attracted to the inside by both the electrical and concentration gradients. Therefore, if the sodium gates were opened, there would be considerable impetus for sodium to flow into the cell.

A neuron may receive input that either hyperpolarizes it (makes the inside more negative) or depolarizes it (makes the inside less negative). If the membrane is depolarized to a threshold level, it briefly loses its ability to exclude sodium ions, and these ions rush in through voltage-activated sodium gates. They cause the inside of the neuron to become positive, at which point the membrane quickly becomes impermeable to sodium again. However, as the neuron becomes more depolarized, voltage activated potassium gates open, and the membrane becomes even more permeable than usual to potassium, which is repelled out of the neuron by both the positive electrical gradient and its own concentration gradient. The exit of the positively charged potassium ions returns the neuron approximately to its previous resting potential. This rapid exchange of ions is called the action potential. All action potentials of a given neuron are approximately equal in size and shape, regardless of the size of the depolarization that gave rise to them. This principle is called the all or none law. For 1 or more milliseconds after an action potential, a neuron is resistant to reexcitation. During the absolute refractory period, no stimulus can initiate a new impulse; during the subsequent relative refractory period, slight hyperpolarization resulting from potassium outflow makes it more difficult, but possible, to produce an action potential.

Once an action potential occurs, entering sodium ions spread to adjacent portions of membrane, thereby depolarizing these areas to their threshold and allowing sodium to rush in there. Thus the action potential is regenerated at each succeeding area of the axon until it reaches the end. The regenerative flow of ions across the membrane is slower than electrical conduction within the axon. In some axons, 1-mm-long segments of myelin (a fatty insulating substance) are wrapped around the axon, with short uncovered segments (nodes of Ranvier) in between. The action potential is conducted passively with some decrement under the myelin sheath. There is still sufficient potential to depolarize the next node of Ranvier to its threshold, and the action potential is regenerated at full strength at each node. The impulse appears to "jump" from node to node. This mode of transmission is called saltatory conduction and is much faster than transmission without myelin. It forces the action potential to use the faster electrical conduction within the axon for a longer distance before engaging in the slower regenerative flow across the membrane. Very small local neurons use only graded potentials, not action potentials, because they transmit information over very short distances.

KEY TERMS AND CONCEPTS

The cells of the nervous system
1. Neurons and glia
    The structures within an animal cell
        Membrane
        Cytoplasm
        Nucleus
        Mitochondria
        Ribosomes
        Endoplasmic reticulum
        Lysosomes
        Golgi complex
    The structure of a neuron
        Cell body or soma
        Dendrites
            Dendritic spines
        Axon
            Axon hillock
            Myelin sheath
            Presynaptic terminal or end bulb
        Synapse
    Variations among neurons
        Receptor or sensory neuron
        Motor or effector neuron
        Interneuron
        Additional terms
            Afferent
            Efferent
            Intrinsic
    Glia
        Form myelin sheaths
            Oligodendrocytes: CNS
            Schwann cells: PNS
        Remove waste, promote growth, kill weak cells
            Microglia
            Astrocytes

13

Fill in space, form scar tissue
    Astroglia
Guide neurons
    Radial glia, during development
    Schwann cells, during regeneration of peripheral axons
Exchange chemicals with neurons
    Astrocytes

2. Changes in the structure of neurons and glia
Neurons
    General inability to divide
        Exceptions: olfactory receptors, areas of rat brain
    Potential for dendritic branching
Glia
    Ability to divide
    Origin of cancer
Alcohol: impairs dendritic branching
Aging: loss of neurons
    Normal old people: increased dendritic branching
    Senile old people: decreased dendritic branching

3. The blood-brain barrier
Why we need a blood-brain barrier
    Natural killer cells
    Virus infected cells
    Antibodies
How the blood-brain barrier works
    Endothelial cells along capillaries
    Chemicals that can cross passively
        Small uncharged molecules
        Fat soluble molecules
    Active transport system
        Glucose
        Amino acids
    Astrocytes

4. The nourishment of vertebrate neurons
Dependence on glucose
    Due to blood-brain barrier
Requirement for thiamine (vitamin B1)

The nerve impulse
1. The resting potential
Fatty membrane with embedded proteins
Polarization

Microelectrode
Selective permeability
  Ion channels, or gates
Sodium-potassium pump
  Active transport
Concentration gradient
Electrical gradient
Why a resting potential? Strong, fast response

2. The action potential
   Hyperpolarization
   Depolarization
   Threshold
   All-or-none law
   Voltage-activated gates
   Sodium inflow
   Potassium outflow
   Drug effects
       Scorpion venom
       Local anesthetic
       General anesthetic
   The refractory period
       Absolute refractory period
       Relative refractory period

3. Propagation of the action potential
   Axon hillock
   Successive depolarization of adjacent areas
   Regenerative ion flow slower than current spread in axon

4. The myelin sheath and saltatory conduction
   Myelinated axons
   Nodes of Ranvier
   Saltatory conduction
   Multiple sclerosis

5. Signaling without action potentials
   Local neuron
   Graded potentials
       Depolarization
       Hyperpolarization

SHORT-ANSWER QUESTIONS

The cells of the nervous system
1. *Neurons and glia*
   a. What did Ramon y Cajal demonstrate?

   b. List the major structures of animal cells and give the main function of each?

   c. What are the main subdivisions of the neuron and the function of each?

   d. List seven anatomical distinctions between dendrites and axons.

   e. What is the myelin sheath?

f.   What is the function of the presynaptic terminal or end bulb?

g.   List the three major types of neurons and tell what each is specialized to do. What is another term for sensory neuron?

h.   What do the terms *afferent* and *efferent* mean? Can an axon be both afferent and efferent? Explain.

i.   What is an intrinsic neuron?

j.   How do glia differ from neurons?

k.   What are four major functions of glia?

l.   What two kinds of glia form myelin sheaths?

m.   When brain damage occurs, what are three functions of microglia and astrocytes?

n.   What is the function of radial glia? What related function do Schwann cells perform?

o.   What kind of glia exchanges chemicals with adjacent neurons?

2. *Changes in the structure of neurons and glia*
   a. What are some exceptions to the general principle that vertebrate neurons are not replaced after they die?

   b. What type of cell is most likely to be involved in brain cancer? Why?

   c. Does the microscopic anatomy of dendrites change in normal adults?

   d. What changes are associated with exposure to alcohol?

   e. How do the brains of normal, alert old people differ from those of middle-aged people? How do the brains of senile old people differ?

3. *The blood-brain barrier*
   a. Why do we need a blood-brain barrier? Why don't we have a similar barrier around other body organs?

   b. What happens if a virus does enter the nervous system?

   c. What is the relationship between endothelial cells and astrocytes in forming the blood-brain barrier?

   d. What types of chemicals can cross the blood-brain barrier freely?

   e. Give one reason why heroin produces stronger effects than does morphine.

f. What is the role of the active transport system? What two types
    of chemicals are transported in this way?

4. *Nourishment of vertebrate neurons*
    a. What is the major fuel of neurons?

    b. What are other fuels that infants' neurons can use?

    c. Why can't most parts of the adult brain use those fuels?

    d. Why is a shortage of glucose usually not a problem?

e. Why is a diet low in thiamine a problem?

The nerve impulse
1. *The resting potential*
   a. What is the composition of the membrane covering the neuron? Describe its structure.

   b. How is the electrical potential across the membrane measured?

   c. What is meant by selective permeability of the membrane? Which chemicals can cross the membrane and which ones cannot?

   d. What is the sodium-potassium pump? How does its exchange of sodium and potassium ions lead directly to a small electrical potential across the membrane?

e. How does the selective permeability of the membrane increase the electrical potential?

f. Describe the competing forces acting on potassium ions? Why don't all the potassium ions surrounding a neuron migrate inside the cell to cancel the negative charge there?

g. What is the advantage of expending energy during the "resting" state to establish concentration gradients for sodium and potassium?

2. *The action potential*
    a. What happens to the electrical potential of a cell if a negative charge is applied? What is this change called?

b. What happens to the potential if a brief, small positive current is applied? What is this change called?

c. What happens to the potential if a threshold depolarization is applied?

d. What is the all-or-none law? How may a neuron signal "greater than"?

e. What does the term "voltage-activated sodium gates" mean?

f. What causes the initial rapid increase in positivity of the action potential? Why doesn't the potential stop at 0 rather than actually reversing polarity?

g. What accounts for the ensuing repolarization? Why does this hyperpolarize slightly, rather than stopping at the previous resting potential ?

h. What effect does scorpion venom have on the membrane?

i. What is the effect of local anesthetic drugs like Novocain and Xylocaine?

j. What is the effect of general anesthetics?

k. What is the absolute refractory period?

l. What is the relative refractory period?

m. How does an action potential propagate down an axon?

n. What is the major advantage of the myelin sheath, and how is this advantage conferred?

o. What is meant by saltatory conduction?

p. In what ways is transmission by local neurons different from the usual conduction by axons? Why is this local transmission restricted to very short distances?

POSTTEST

Multiple-Choice Questions

1. The membrane of a cell consists primarily of
   a. two layers of protein molecules.
   b. two layers of fat molecules.
   c. two layers of carbohydrate molecules.
   d. one layer of fat molecules adjacent to a layer of protein molecules.

2. Which of the following is the site of protein synthesis in cells?
   a. nucleus.
   b. mitochondria.
   c. ribosomes.
   d. lysosomes.

3. Which of the following is the site of chemical reactions that produce energy for the cell?
   a. nucleus.
   b. mitochondria.
   c. ribosomes.
   d. lysosomes.

4. Which part of the neuron is specialized to carry electrical activity toward the cell body?
   a. dendrites.
   b. soma.
   c. axon.
   d. end bulbs.

5. Receptor neurons
   a. are sometimes called efferent neurons.
   b. are highly sensitive to specific types of stimulation.
   c. have dendrites and axons that reside entirely within a sensory structure.
   d. more than one of the above.

6. Intrinsic neurons
   a. are afferent to a given structure.
   b. are efferent to a given structure.
   c. have dendrites and axons confined within a structure.
   d. have multiple axons extending to numerous structures.

7. Glia
    a. are larger as well as more numerous than neurons.
    b. are found only surrounding blood vessels in the brain.
    c. are unable to divide.
    d. are unable to form synaptic connections with neurons and other glial cells.

8. Which of the following is *not* a function of glia?
    a. guiding the migration of neurons and the growth of their axons and dendrites
    b. exchanging chemicals with adjacent neurons
    c. forming myelin sheaths
    d. transmitting information to other cells

9. Which of the following functions is *not* performed by glia after brain damage?
    a. forming new neurons by the process of cell division
    b. removing waste material from dead neurons
    c. releasing chemicals that promote growth of remaining healthy neurons
    d. releasing chemicals, such as nitric oxide, that hasten the death of weakened cells

10. Senility and exposure to alcohol are associated with
    a. deficiencies in dendritic branching.
    b. increased dendritic branching.
    c. increased numbers of glia.
    d. deficient patterns of axon branching.

11. The blood-brain barrier
    a. is formed by Schwann cells.
    b. allows some substances to pass freely, others to pass poorly, and still others to not pass through at all.
    c. is completely impermeable to all substances.
    d. keeps the blood from washing away neurons.

12. Which of the following is true of the blood-brain barrier?
    a. Electrically charged molecules are the only molecules that can cross.
    b. Fat soluble molecules cannot cross at all.
    c. It results from the tight junctions between endothelial cells.
    d. An active transport system pumps blood across the barrier.

13. If a virus enters the brain,
    a. it survives in the infected neuron.
    b. a particle of it is exposed through the neuron's membrane so that the infected cell can be killed.
    c. it is immediately removed by glia before it can enter a neuron.
    d. it is impossible for any virus ever to enter the brain.

14. Adult neurons
    a. are like all other cells of the body in depending heavily on glucose.
    b. depend heavily on glucose because they do not have enzymes to metabolize other nutrients.
    c. depend heavily on glucose because other nutrients cannot cross the blood-brain barrier in significant amounts.
    d. cannot use glucose because they do not receive enough oxygen or thiamine through the blood-brain barrier to metabolize it.

15. Potassium
    a. is found mostly outside the neuron.
    b. is pumped into the resting neuron by the sodium-potassium pump, but some flows out as a result of the concentration gradient.
    c. is actively pumped outside the neuron during the action potential.
    d. more than one of the above.

16. The sodium-potassium pump
    a. creates a negative potential inside the neuron by removing 3 sodium ions for every 2 potassium ions that it brings in.
    b. creates a negative potential inside the neuron by removing 2 sodium ions for every 3 potassium ions that it brings in.
    c. creates a positive potential inside the neuron by removing 3 sodium ions for every 2 potassium ions that it brings in.
    d. is basically a passive mechanism that requires no metabolic energy.

17. The resting potential
    a. prepares the neuron to respond rapidly to a stimulus.
    b. is negative inside the neuron relative to the outside.
    c. can be measured by comparing the voltage of two electrodes, one inside and one outside the neuron.
    d. all of the above.

18. Sodium ions
    a. are found largely inside the neuron during the resting state because they are attracted in by the negative charge there.
    b. are found largely inside the neuron during the resting state because they are actively pumped in.
    c. are found largely outside the neuron during the resting state because they are actively pumped out, and the membrane is largely impermeable to their reentry.
    d. are actively repelled by the electrical charge of the neuron's resting potential.

19. Hyperpolarization
    a. refers to a shift in the cell's potential in a more negative direction.
    b. refers to a shift in the cell's potential in a positive direction.
    c. can trigger an action potential if it is large enough.
    d. occurs in an all-or-none fashion.

20. Depolarization of a neuron can be accomplished by having
    a. a negative ion, such as chloride (Cl^-), flow into the cell.
    b. potassium (K^+) ions flow out of the cell.
    c. sodium (Na^+) ions flow into the cell.
    d. sodium ions flow out of the cell.

21. The all-or-none law
    a. applies only to potentials in dendrites.
    b. states that the size and shape of the action potential are independent of the stimulus that initiated it.
    c. makes it impossible for the nervous system to signal intensity of a stimulus.
    d. more than one of the above.

22. When a neuron receives a threshold depolarization
    a. the membrane becomes highly permeable to sodium ions for a brief time.
    b. so much sodium comes in that it almost completely depletes the extracellular fluid of sodium.
    c. sodium flows in only until the potential across the membrane is zero.
    d. an action potential occurs, the size of which reflects the size of the stimulus that gave rise to it.

23. The down slope of the action potential graph
    a. is largely a result of sodium ions being pumped back out again.
    b. is the result of potassium ions flowing in briefly.
    c. is the result of sodium ions flowing in briefly.
    d. usually passes the level of the resting potential, resulting in a brief hyperpolarization due to potassium freely leaving the cell.

24. Which of the following is true?
    a. Local anesthetics block nerve transmission by blocking sodium gates.
    b. Scorpion venom also blocks sodium gates.
    c. General anesthetics keep sodium channels open and close potassium channels.
    d. All of the above are true.

25. The absolute refractory period
    a. is the time during which a stimulus must exceed the usual threshold in order to produce an action potential.
    b. is the time during which a neuron is more excitable than usual.
    c. sets a maximum on the firing frequency of a neuron.
    d. more than one of the above.

26. Propagation of an action potential
    a. is analogous to the flow of electrons down a wire.
    b. is almost instantaneous.
    c. is inherently unidirectional because positive charges can flow only in one direction.
    d. depends on passive diffusion of sodium ions inside the axon, which depolarize the neighboring areas.

27. Myelin sheaths
    a. are interrupted about every 1 mm by a short unmyelinated segment.
    b. would be much more efficient if they were not interrupted with a lot of leaky nodes.
    c. are less effective in speeding transmission than a simple increase in axon size.
    d. none of the above.

28. Saltatory conduction refers to
    a. the salt ions used in the action potential.
    b. the jumping in of sodium ions once the sodium gates are opened.
    c. the impulse jumping from one node of Ranvier to the next.
    d. the impulse jumping from one myelin sheath to the next.

29. Myelin sheaths
    a. slow conduction of the impulse by blocking sodium's entry to the cell; their advantage lies in making the impulse all or none.
    b. are destroyed in multiple sclerosis.
    c. are found on dendrites.
    d. are found on cell bodies.

30. The nodes of Ranvier
    a. are interruptions of the myelin sheath at about 1 mm intervals.
    b. are sites of abundant sodium gates.
    c. are sites where an action potential is regenerated.
    d. all of the above.

31. Local neurons utilize
    a. action potentials to transmit information over long distances.
    b. action potentials to transmit information over short distances.
    c. graded potentials to convey information over short distances.
    d. graded potentials to convey information over long distances.

Answers to Multiple-Choice Questions

1. b	7. d	13. a	19. a	25. c	31. c
2. c	8. d	14. c	20. c	26. d	
3. b	9. a	15. b	21. b	27. a	
4. a	10. a	16. a	22. a	28. c	
5. b	11. b	17. d	23. d	29. b	
6. c	12. c	18. c	24. a	30. d	

Diagrams

1. Label the following structures on the diagram of a motor neuron below: axon, axon hillock, dendrites, myelin sheath, node of Ranvier, nucleus, soma, presynaptic terminals, muscle fiber.

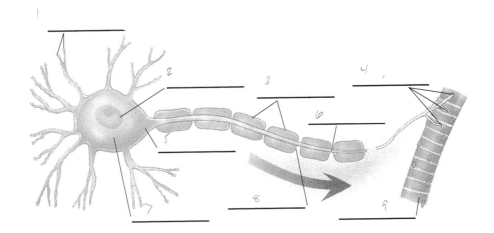

2. Label the four types of glia pictured below.

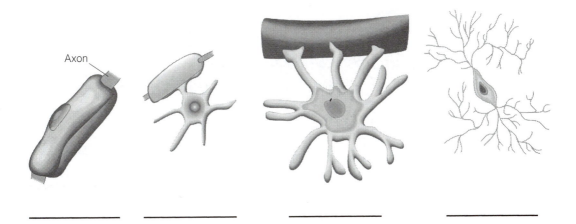

3. Label the blanks below as either Na⁺ or K⁺.

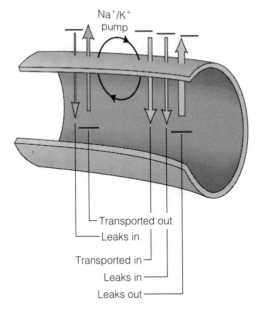

Na⁺/K⁺ pump

Transported out
Leaks in
Transported in
Leaks in
Leaks out

4. Label the electrical potentials shown in the graph below.

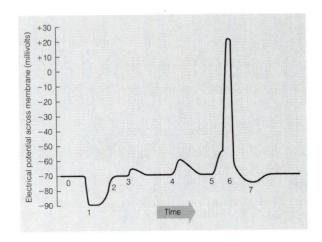

0 _____   4 _____

1 _____   5 _____

2 _____   6 _____

3 _____   7 _____

3

SYNAPSES AND DRUGS

INTRODUCTION

C. S. Sherrington inferred from careful behavioral observations that neurons do not merge with each other but communicate across tiny gaps called synapses. Reflex arcs that have one or more synapses are slower than simple transmission along the same distance of unbroken axon. Sherrington also inferred that complex integration of stimuli, including spatial and temporal summation of both excitation and inhibition, occurs at synapses. Most of his inferences were later confirmed by electrophysiological recordings using microelectrodes inserted inside neurons. Inhibitory postsynaptic potentials (IPSPs) hyperpolarize the postsynaptic cell, making it more difficult to produce an action potential. Excitatory postsynaptic potentials (EPSPs) depolarize the postsynaptic neuron and may summate spatially and temporally with other EPSPs to reach triggering threshold for an action potential.

EPSPs and IPSPs result from the release of neurotransmitters from presynaptic terminals. The neurotransmitter diffuses to and combines with receptor sites on the postsynaptic neuron, giving rise to either ionotropic or metabotropic changes that produce the postsynaptic potentials. The neurotransmitter then detaches from its receptor and is either reabsorbed by the presynaptic terminal and reused or broken by enzymes into inactive components. Different neurotransmitters have different modes of inactivation, but some form of inactivation is critical to prevent the neurotransmitter from having a prolonged effect on the postsynaptic neuron and making it incapable of responding to new stimuli. The effect on the postsynaptic cell depends on the type and amount of neurotransmitter, the nature and number of receptors, the amount of deactivating enzyme present at the synapse, the rate of reuptake, and probably other factors. Neuromodulators are substances that alter the effects of neurotransmitters at nearby cells, frequently having no effect by themselves. Each neuron is thought to release the same neurotransmitter or combination of neurotransmitters at all of its terminals. Although each particular synapse is always excitatory or always inhibitory, each neuron receives many synapses, some of which are excitatory and some of which are inhibitory. Some synaptic mechanisms involve a brief flow of ions; others affect metabolic processes and are of slower onset and longer duration. However, all neurotransmitters must be inactivated, either by reuptake into presynaptic terminals or by enzymes. The most widely studied neurotransmitter systems are those of acetylcholine, dopamine, norepinephrine, epinephrine, serotonin, glycine, gamma-aminobutyric acid, beta-endorphin, and the enkephalins. Levels of some neurotransmitters can be affected by diet.

Drugs typically either impede or facilitate chemical transmission at a given type of synapse. They may either block or activate a certain type of receptor, or they may affect release, reuptake, or enzyme inactivation of the neurotransmitter. Since different neurotransmitters have different behavioral and physiological effects, we can frequently predict the effect of a drug on behavior or physiology if we know its synaptic effect. Some stimulant drugs, such as amphetamine and cocaine, primarily increase activity at dopamine synapses. However, the stimulant effects of caffeine result from dilation of blood vessels and from blocking inhibitory adenosine receptors on glutamate terminals; as a result, the release of the excitatory neurotransmitter glutamate is increased. Nicotine stimulates nicotinic acetylcholine receptors, thereby increasing heart rate and blood pressure; the reason that it stimulates some people and relaxes others is not fully understood. Opiates stimulate receptors that are normally activated by endorphins; they result indirectly in an increase in dopamine release, which may explain their addictive property. Marijuana stimulates cannabinoid receptors, which are located primarily in the hippocampus, basal ganglia, and cerebellum. Hallucinogenic drugs stimulate the $5\text{-}HT_2$ subtype of serotonin receptor. Alcohol produces general effects on membranes, but also increases activity at $GABA_A$ receptors. There are many individual differences in responsiveness to drugs and many effects that we do not understand.

KEY TERMS AND CONCEPTS

The concept of the synapse
1. The properties of synapses
    Charles Sherrington's inferences
        Reflex
        Coordinated flexing and extending
        Synaptic delay
        Temporal summation
        Spatial summation
    John Eccles
        Microelectrode
        Excitatory postsynaptic potential (EPSP)
        Inhibitory postsynaptic potential (IPSP)

2. Relationship among EPSP, IPSP, and action potential
    Spontaneous firing rate

3. The neuronal decision process
    Disinhibition

Chemical events at the synapse

1. Discovery that most synaptic transmission is chemical
    - T. R. Elliott
        - Adrenalin
        - Sympathetic nervous system
    - O. Loewi
        - Vagus nerve
        - "Accelerator" nerve

2. The sequence of chemical events at a synapse
    - Types of neurotransmitters
        - Biogenic amines
        - Amino acids
        - Peptides
        - Nitric oxide
    - Synthesis of transmitters
        - Role of diet
        - Acetylcholine
            - Choline
        - Dopamine, norepinephrine, epinephrine
            - Catecholamines
            - Phenylalanine and tyrosine
        - Serotonin
            - Tryptophan
            - Role of insulin
    - Transport of transmitters
    - Release and diffusion
        - Voltage-dependent calcium gates
        - Quantum
        - Vesicles
        - Nonvesicular release
        - Combination of transmitters
    - Activation of receptors of the postsynaptic cell
        - Ionotropic effects (rapid, short-lived)
            - Glutamate
            - GABA
            - Acetylcholine (nicotinic)
        - Metabotropic effects and "second messenger" systems (slow)
            - G-protein (coupled to GTP)
            - Cyclic AMP
            - Biogenic amines
        - Neuromodulators, including peptides
            - Conditional effect
    - Presynaptic receptors
        - Autoreceptor

Inactivation and reuptake
    Acetylcholinesterase
        Reuptake
        COMT (catechol-o-methyltransferase)
        MAO (monoamine oxidase)

3. Neurotransmitters and behavior
    Multiple receptor types

Synapses, drugs, and behavior
1. How drugs can affect synapses
    Effects on presynaptic neuron
        Increase or decrease synthesis
        Increase or decrease release
        Stimulate or block presynaptic receptors
    Effects on postsynaptic neuron
        Agonist
        Antagonist
        Affinity
    Effects on events after transmission
        Block reabsorption
        Block inactivation
    Complications
        Multiple receptor types
        Multiple effects

2. Modes of action of stimulant drugs
    Amphetamine and cocaine
        D_2 and D_3 dopamine receptors
        Acetylcholine (opposing effects)
        D_1 dopamine receptors
        Rebound "crash"
        "Crack" (freebase cocaine)
            Faster access to brain
    Caffeine
        Dilates blood vessels, increases heart rate and blood flow
        Interferes with adenosine
            Presynaptic receptors
            Indirectly increases glutamate release
    Nicotine
        Effects on heart rate, blood pressure, breathing rate
        Nicotinic acetylcholine receptors
        Curare

3. Other commonly abused drugs
- Opiates
  - Morphine, heroin, methadone
  - Endorphins
  - Decrease GABA release
  - Indirectly increase dopamine release
- Marijuana
  - Cannabinoids
    - Tetrahydrocannabinol (THC)
    - Dissolve in body fats, remain in body
    - Cannabinoid receptors
      - Hippocampus, basal ganglia, cerebellum
      - Absent from brain stem
    - Anandamide
- Hallucinogenic drugs
  - LSD, PCP, mescaline and
  - 5-HT$_2$ serotonin receptors
- Alcohol
  - Membrane effects
  - GABA$_A$ receptor
  - Several genetic predispositions
    - "General addiction"
    - Alcohol metabolism
      - Acetaldehyde
      - Acetaldehyde dehydrogenase
      - Acetic acid
      - Antabuse (disulfiram)

SHORT-ANSWER QUESTIONS

The concept of the synapse
1. *The properties of synapses*
   a. What is a reflex?

b.   What experimental evidence did Sherrington have for synaptic delay? for temporal summation?

c.   What evidence did he have for spatial summation? for coordinated excitation and inhibition?

d.   Describe John Eccles's experimental support for Sherrington's inferences.

e.   What is an EPSP, and what ionic flow is largely responsible for it?

f.   What is an IPSP, and what ionic flows can produce it?

2. *The relationship among EPSP, IPSP, and action potential*
    a. Why may some synapses have a greater influence than others?

    b. What influence do EPSPs and IPSPs have on neurons with a spontaneous rate of firing?

3. *The neuronal decision process*
    a. What factors influence a cell's "decision" whether or not to produce an action potential?

Chemical events at the synapse
1. *Discovery that most synaptic transmission is chemical*
    a. What did T. R. Elliott propose?

    b. Describe Loewi's experiment with the frog's heart.

2. *Sequence of chemical events at a synapse*
   a. What are the six major events, in sequence, at a synapse?

   b. List the major neurotransmitters.

   c. How is nitric oxide unlike most other neurotransmitters?

   d. How is the synthesis of peptide neurotransmitters different from that of most other neurotransmitters?

   e. List the three catecholamines in the order of their synthesis. What determines which one will be released by a given neuron?

f. How might one increase the amount of acetylcholine in the brain? the catecholamines? serotonin?

g. How quickly can neurotransmitter molecules be transported down the axon to the terminal? Why is this a special problem for peptide neurotransmitters?

h. What is a quantum? Give one physical basis for quantal release of transmitter. Why has the vesicle hypothesis been questioned?

i. What generalization can be drawn regarding the release of various transmitters at the terminals of a given neuron?

j. Contrast ionotropic and metabotropic synaptic mechanisms. List three ionotropic neurotransmitters.

k. Discuss the role of "second messengers" in producing the metabotropic effects of transmitters.

l. What is a G-protein? What is the "first messenger"? What is one common second messenger?

m. What is a neuromodulator? How does a neuromodulator differ from most neurotransmitters?

n. What is the function of presynaptic receptors? What is an autoreceptor?

o. How are ACh, 5-HT, and the catecholamines inactivated? Why is inactivation important?

3. *Neurotransmitters and behavior*

a. Why should there be multiple receptor types for each neurotransmitter?

Synapses, drugs, and behavior
1. *How drugs can affect synapses*
    a. List eight ways in which drugs may affect synaptic action.

    b. What is an agonist? an antagonist?

    c. How can one drug be an agonist at a given receptor, while another drug, with similar affinity for that receptor, is an antagonist?

    d. What is the effect of the drug AMPT (alpha-methyl-para-tyrosine)?

45

e.   What is the effect of amphetamine on synapses? on psychological state?

f.   Compare the effects of cocaine with those of amphetamine. What are the similarities and differences?

g.   Why do amphetamine and cocaine users frequently report a "crash" a couple of hours after taking the drugs?

h.   Which neurotransmitter appears to be especially important for the addictive property of drugs? Which neurotransmitter seems to have opposing effects?

i.   How does caffeine stimulate the nervous system? What is a major effect of adenosine?

j.   What type of receptor does nicotine stimulate? What are its effects on heart rate and blood pressure? What is the main physiological effect of curare?

k.   What is an endorphin? How were endorphins discovered? What may account for opiates' addictive property?

l.   What is the main psychoactive chemical in marijuana? Why do marijuana users not experience a sudden "crash" several hours after taking the drug, as do amphetamine and cocaine users?

m.   Where in the brain are cannabinoid receptors located? What is the endogenous chemical that binds to them?

n.   Which receptor does LSD stimulate? Can we explain the effects of LSD on behavior?

o. What are two effects of alcohol on membranes? What type of receptor is made more responsive by alcohol?

p. Describe the metabolism of alcohol. What are two reasons why Antabuse (disulfiram) may inhibit drinking?

POSTTEST

Multiple-Choice Questions

1. C. S. Sherrington
    a. did extensive electrophysiological recording of synaptic events.
    b. inferred the existence and properties of synapses from behavioral experiments on reflexes in dogs.
    c. was a student of John Eccles.
    d. found that conduction along a single axon is slower than through a reflex arc.

2. Which of the following was *not* one of Sherrington's findings?
    a. The speed of conduction through a reflex arc was significantly slower than the known speed of conduction along an axon.
    b. Repeating a subthreshold pinch several times in rapid succession elicited leg flexion.
    c. Simultaneous subthreshold pinches in different parts of the foot elicited flexion.
    d. Reflex arcs are limited to one limb and are always excitatory.

3. Electrophysiological recording from a single neuron
    a. utilizes a microelectrode inserted into the neuron.
    b. supported Sherrington's inferences.
    c. is a field pioneered by John Eccles.
    d. all of the above.

4. IPSPs
    a. may summate to generate an action potential.
    b. are always hyperpolarizing under natural conditions.
    c. are characterized mainly by an influx of sodium ions.
    d. are characterized by a large influx of sodium and a smaller influx of potassium.

5. Which of the following is true?
    a. The size of EPSPs is the same at all excitatory synapses.
    b. The primary means of inactivation of synaptic potentials for all transmitter substances is degradation by an enzyme.
    c. The size, duration, and direction (that is, hyperpolarizing or depolarizing) of a postsynaptic potential are functions of the type and amount of transmitter released, the type and number of receptor sites present, the amount of deactivating enzyme present at the synapse, the rate of reuptake, and perhaps other factors.
    d. A given neuron may release either an excitatory or an inhibitory transmitter (at different times), depending on whether it was excited or inhibited by a previous neuron.

6. EPSPs and action potentials are *similar* in that
    a. sodium is the major ion producing a depolarization in both.
    b. sodium is the major ion producing a hyperpolarization in both.
    c. potassium is the major ion producing a depolarization in both.
    d. both decay as a function of time and space and decrease in magnitude as they travel along the membrane.

7. EPSPs
    a. result from a flow of potassium (K^+) and chloride (Cl^-) ions.
    b. are always depolarizing in natural conditions.
    c. are always large enough to cause the postsynaptic cell to reach triggering threshold for an action potential; otherwise there would be too much uncertainty in the nervous system.
    d. are the same as action potentials.

8. EPSPs and IPSPs
    a. may alter a neuron's spontaneous firing rate.
    b. are more effective if they are located at the end of dendrites, rather than on the cell body.
    c. usually occur one at a time, so that the neuron does not get "confused."
    d. all of the above.

9. T. R. Elliott discovered that
   a. adrenalin slowed a frog's heart.
   b. adrenalin could mimic the effects of the sympathetic nervous system.
   c. synaptic transmission is electrical rather than chemical.
   d. all of the above.

10. Otto Loewi discovered that a substance collected from the vagus nerve innervating one frog's heart and transferred to a second frog's heart
    a. slowed the second frog's heart.
    b. altered electrical conduction of the second frog's heart so it could no longer beat.
    c. either speeded or slowed the second frog's heart, depending on the quantity applied.
    d. speeded the second frog's heart.

11. The level of acetylcholine in the brain can be increased by increasing dietary intake of
    a. acetylcholine.
    b. tyrosine.
    c. choline.
    d. tryptophan.

12. The level of serotonin in the brain can be increased by eating a meal that has protein and is also high in
    a. choline.
    b. tyrosine.
    c. protein.
    d. carbohydrates.

13. The speed of transport of substances down an axon
    a. is fast enough that even the longest axons require only a few minutes for substances synthesized in the nucleus to reach the terminal.
    b. limits the availability of acetylcholine and the catecholamines more than that of peptides.
    c. limits the availability of peptides more than that of acetylcholine and the catecholamines.
    d. is a severe limitation on the availability of all neurotransmitters.

14. Calcium
    a. is kept outside the neuron by voltage-dependent calcium gates when the membrane is at rest.
    b. enters the terminal when the voltage-dependent calcium gates are opened by an action potential.
    c. causes the release of neurotransmitter.
    d. all of the above.

15. Vesicles
    a. are near-spherical packets filled with neurotransmitter.
    b. store all of the transmitter in the terminal.
    c. are now considered to be the only anatomical basis for the quantal release of transmitter.
    d. store only excitatory neurotransmitters; inhibitory neurotransmitters are never stored in vesicles.

16. Each terminal of a given axon
    a. releases a different combination of neurotransmitters in order to provide a rich repertoire of effects.
    b. releases the same neurotransmitter or combination of neurotransmitters as every other terminal of that axon.
    c. releases only one neurotransmitter, so as not to "confuse" the postsynaptic cell.
    d. releases all of the neurotransmitters known to exist in the brain.

17. Ionotropic synaptic mechanisms
    a. have slow-onset, long-lasting effects.
    b. use a cyclic AMP response.
    c. are exemplified by acetylcholine (at nicotinic receptors), glutamate, and GABA.
    d. frequently use hormones as transmitters.

18. Metabotropic synapses
    a. may have effects that significantly outlast the release of transmitter.
    b. are exemplified by at least some epinephrine synapses.
    c. are characterized by initiation of changes in proteins by cyclic AMP, which in turn open or close ion gates or alter the structure or metabolism of the cell.
    d. all of the above.

19. Neuromodulators
    a. frequently have an effect only when the "main" neurotransmitter is present.
    b. are carried in the blood throughout the entire body.
    c. almost always produce a major effect by themselves, in addition to their modulatory effect.
    d. usually have ionotropic effects.

20. Acetylcholinesterase
    a. promotes reuptake of ACh into cholinergic terminals, thereby inactivating it.
    b. is the enzyme that produces ACh.
    c. is the enzyme that cleaves ACh into two inactive parts.
    d. blocks reuptake of choline into cholinergic terminals.

21. Reuptake of neurotransmitter
    a. is the major method of inactivation of ACh.
    b. is the major method of inactivation of serotonin and the catecholamines.
    c. is speeded up by COMT.
    d. is completely blocked by MAO.

22. An antagonist is a drug that
    a. has no affinity for a receptor.
    b. changes EPSPs into IPSPs.
    c. mimics or strengthens the effects of a neurotransmitter.
    d. blocks the effects of a neurotransmitter.

23. Amphetamine
    a. stimulates the release of dopamine and norepinephrine.
    b. blocks the conversion of tyrosine to dopa.
    c. stimulates adenosine receptors.
    d. stimulates nicotinic receptors.

24. Cocaine
    a. increases total activity throughout the brain.
    b. blocks reuptake of norepinephrine and dopamine.
    c. is absorbed into fat, especially in the form of "crack" cocaine, and released slowly, thereby preventing a "crash" a few hours later.
    d. all of the above.

25. Caffeine
    a. constricts blood vessels.
    b. stimulates adenosine receptors.
    c. indirectly increases the release of glutamate.
    d. directly decreases the release of glutamate.

26. Nicotine
    a. stimulates nicotinic receptors.
    b. blocks nicotinic receptors.
    c. blocks dopamine receptors.
    d. is used on arrows by South American Indians to cause paralysis.

27. Opiates
    a. block receptors that are stimulated by endorphins.
    b. inhibit GABA neurons and thereby increase dopamine release.
    c. inhibit dopamine neurons and thereby increase GABA release.
    d. are especially addictive when taken for medical reasons.

28. Marijuana
    a. stimulates cannabinoid receptors located primarily in the brain stem; it thereby interferes with breathing.
    b. blocks adenosine receptors.
    c. is very likely to produce a "crash" a couple of hours after its ingestion.
    d. mimics the effects of the endogenous neurotransmitter anandamide.

29. LSD
    a. stimulates the release of norepinephrine and dopamine.
    b. blocks most serotonin receptors.
    c. is an agonist at $5\text{-}HT_2$ receptors.
    d. blocks the synthesis of serotonin.

30. Alcohol
    a. inhibits the flow of sodium across the membrane.
    b. expands the surface of all membranes.
    c. makes $GABA_A$ receptors more responsive.
    d. all of the above.

31. Acetaldehyde dehydrogenase
    a. is the generic name for Antabuse.
    b. controls the rate of conversion of acetic acid, a toxic product of alcohol metabolism, into acetaldehyde, a source of energy.
    c. controls the rate of conversion of acetaldehyde, a toxic product of alcohol metabolism, into acetic acid, a source of energy.
    d. is controlled primarily by a "general, all-purpose addiction gene."

Answers to Multiple-Choice Questions

1. b	6. a	11. c	16. b	21. b	26. a
2. d	7. b	12. d	17. c	22. d	27. b
3. d	8. a	13. c	18. d	23. a	28. d
4. b	9. b	14. d	19. a	24. b	29. c
5. c	10. a	15. a	20. c	25. c	30. d
					31. c

Diagram

Judging from the indicated movement of ions, which synapse is excitatory and which is inhibitory? Label the components of the synapse.

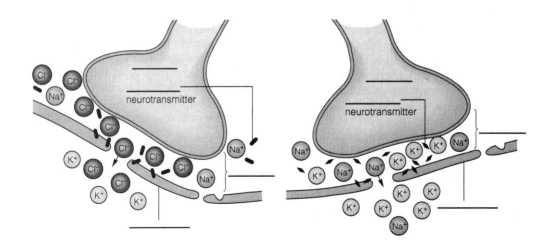

4

ANATOMY OF THE NERVOUS SYSTEM
AND METHODS OF INVESTIGATION

INTRODUCTION

The vertebrate nervous system consists of two major divisions, the central (CNS) and the peripheral (PNS) nervous systems. The CNS is composed of the brain and the spinal cord. The PNS is divided into the somatic and the autonomic nervous systems. The somatic system consists of sensory nerves that convey information from sense organs to the spinal cord, and motor nerves carrying messages from the spinal cord to muscles and glands. A pair of sensory nerves enters (one from each side) and a pair of motor nerves exits from the spinal cord through each pair of openings in the vertebral canal. The sensory nerves enter the spinal cord from the dorsal side, and the motor axons leave from the ventral side. Cell bodies of sensory neurons lie in the dorsal root ganglia; those of the motor neurons are in the spinal cord. The autonomic nervous system also sends neurons through the vertebral openings, to synapse in ganglia outside the spinal cord. Ganglia of the sympathetic division of the autonomic nervous system are arranged in an interconnected chain along the thoracic and lumbar sections of the spinal cord. Ganglia of the parasympathetic division receive input from the cranial nerves and the sacral section of the cord and are located near the organs they innervate. The interconnections of the sympathetic system promote unified action by the body in a fight-or-flight situation, whereas the relative independence of the parasympathetic innervations allows for more discrete energy-saving responses. Most of the final synapses of the sympathetic nervous system use the neurotransmitter norepinephrine, while the final parasympathetic synapses use acetylcholine.

The brain is divided into the hindbrain, the midbrain, and the forebrain. The hindbrain is composed of the medulla, the pons, and the cerebellum. The medulla contains numerous nuclei that control life-preserving reflexes; the pons has many fibers that cross from right to left, going to the cerebellum, which is directly behind the pons. The cerebellum helps control motor coordination. The reticular formation, which is important for arousal, and the raphe system, which helps regulate sleep, have diffusely branching neurons throughout the medulla, pons, and midbrain. The midbrain is composed of the tectum (or roof), on which are the two superior colliculi and the two inferior colliculi, involved in sensory processing; and the tegmentum, containing extensions of neural systems of the hindbrain. The forebrain includes the hypothalamus, important for motivational and hormonal regulation; the pituitary or master gland; the basal ganglia, which influence motor movements; the hippocampus, important in memory functions; the thalamus, which is the main source of input to the cerebral cortex; and the cerebral cortex, which surrounds the rest of the brain and is responsible for complex sensory analysis and integration, language processing, motor control, and social awareness. The ventricles are fluid-filled cavities within the brain.

The cerebral cortex consists of up to six laminae, or layers, of cell bodies parallel to the surface of the brain. The cells are organized into columns, perpendicular to the laminae; each column contains cells with similar response properties. The occipital lobe of the cerebral cortex is the site of primary visual processing. The parietal lobe processes somatosensory information and contributes to several complex processes, including identification of objects by touch, body image, and ability to use maps. The temporal lobe processes auditory information and is important for perception of complex visual patterns and comprehension of language. The frontal lobe contains the motor cortex, which controls fine movements, and prefrontal cortex, which contributes to an internal representation of the world and social awareness.

Since the brain is incredibly complex, we must use a variety of techniques to understand its function. Small areas of the brain may be stimulated or damaged, using a stereotaxic instrument and atlas for guidance; location is later confirmed by histological techniques. One method is to make a lesion in a given structure; the resulting behavioral deficits must then be described as precisely and comprehensively as possible. A brain structure involved with control of movement or motivation may be investigated by electrical stimulation and recording, coupled with careful behavioral observation. It is possible to label metabolic activity using autoradiography and to measure the distribution of a chemical using immunohistochemistry. Additional methods include study of animals with genetic lesions or arrested development and correlation of development of brain and behavior. The structure of living human brains can be assessed using computerized axial tomography (CAT) or magnetic resonance imaging (MRI). Human brain activity can be inferred from the electroencephalograph (EEG), from positron-emission tomography (PET), and from records of regional cerebral blood flow.

KEY TERMS AND CONCEPTS

Basic subdivisions of the vertebrate nervous system
1. The spinal cord and its communication with the periphery
    Sensory nerves
    Motor nerves
    Bell-Magendie Law
    Dorsal root ganglion

Spinal nerves
Dermatome
Gray matter
White matter

2. The autonomic nervous system
    Sympathetic nervous system ("fight or flight")
        Sympathetic chain of ganglia
        Thoracic and lumbar regions
        Norepinephrine
    Parasympathetic nervous system (energy conserving)
        Cranial and sacral regions
        Ganglia near organs
        Acetylcholine

3. The hindbrain
    Brain stem
    Medulla
        Vital reflexes
        Cranial nerves
    Pons ("bridge")
        Fibers crossing
        Cranial nerves
    Reticular formation
    Raphe system
    Cerebellum

4. The midbrain
    Tectum
        Superior and inferior colliculi
    Tegmentum
        Substantia nigra

5. The forebrain
    Hypothalamus
    Pituitary gland
    Basal ganglia
        Caudate nucleus
        Putamen
        Globus pallidus
    Hippocampus
        Fornix
        Fimbria
    Thalamus

6. The ventricles
    Central canal
    Cerebrospinal fluid (CSF)
    Subarachnoid space
    Hydrocephalus

The cerebral cortex
1. Organization of the cerebral cortex
    Laminae and columns
    Sensory, motor, and association areas

2. Occipital lobe
    Primary visual cortex
        Striate cortex
        Cortical blindness

3. Parietal lobe
    Central sulcus
    Postcentral gyrus
    Primary somatosensory cortex
        Two light-touch bands
        One deep-pressure band
        One light-touch and deep-pressure band
    Effects of damage
        Impaired identification of objects by touch
        Clumsiness on opposite side of body
        Neglect of opposite side of body
        Distortion of body image
        Inability to draw and follow maps

4. Temporal lobe
    Primary auditory cortex
    Complex visual patterns
    Language comprehension
    Klüver-Bucy syndrome

5. Frontal lobe
    Primary motor cortex
        Precentral gyrus
    Prefrontal cortex
        Prefrontal lobotomies
            Lack of initiative
            Failure to inhibit unacceptable impulses
            Impairment of some aspects of memory
            Impaired facial expression of emotion

Internal representation of the world
 Delayed response task
 Object permanence

Methods of investigating how the brain controls behavior
 Phrenology -- pseudoscience
1. The stereotaxic instrument
 Bregma
 Stereotaxic atlas

2. Lesions and ablations
 Sham lesion
 Histological techniques
  Microtome
  Stains
 Difficulties in interpreting lesion experiments
  Double dissociation of function

3. Stimulation of and recording from the brain
 Implanted electrodes

4. Labeling brain activity
 Autoradiography
  Radioactive 2-deoxy-D-glucose
  Radioactive amino acids
 Immunohistochemistry

5. Studies using natural development of the brain
 Genetic lesions and arrested development
 Correlating developing brain with behavior

6. Studies of the structure of living human brains
 Computerized axial tomography (CT or CAT)
 Magnetic resonance imaging (MRI)
  Nuclear magnetic resonance (NMR)
  Echo-planar MRI

7. Measurement of human brain activity
 Electroencephalograph (EEG)
  Evoked potential
 Positron-emission tomography (PET)
 Regional cerebral blood flow (rCBF)
  Potassium ions
  Nitric oxide

SHORT-ANSWER QUESTIONS

Basic subdivisions of the vertebrate nervous system
1. *The spinal cord and its communication with the periphery*
   a. Draw a cross section of the spinal cord, including sensory and motor nerves, dorsal root ganglion, and dorsal and ventral directions.

   b. What is the Bell-Magendie Law?

   c. Why is white matter white? Of what does it consist?

2. *The autonomic nervous system*
   a. Of what two parts does the autonomic nervous system consist? Give the location and basic function of each.

   b. Which transmitter is used by the postganglionic parasympathetic nerves? Which is used by most sympathetic postganglionic nerves?

3. *The hindbrain*
   a. What are the three components of the hindbrain? Give one "specialty" of each.

   b. List the 12 cranial nerves and note their sensory and/or motor function.

   c. What are the anatomical location and functions of the reticular formation and the raphe system?

4. *The midbrain*
   a. What are the two major divisions of the midbrain? Name two structures in each division.

5. *The forebrain*
   a. Where is the hypothalamus, and what kinds of behavior does it help regulate?

b.	Where is the pituitary? What is its function? What structure largely controls it?

c.	Where are the basal ganglia? Which structures make up the basal ganglia? Briefly describe their function.

d.	Where is the hippocampus? What psychological process has it been linked to?

e.	Describe the relationship of the thalamus to the cerebral cortex.

6.	*The ventricles*
	a.	What are the ventricles? Where is cerebrospinal fluid (CSF) formed? In which direction does it flow? Where is it reabsorbed into blood vessels?

b.   What are the functions of CSF?

The cerebral cortex
1.   *Organization of cerebral cortex*
   a.   What is the relationship of gray matter to white in the cortex?
         Compare this relationship to that in the spinal cord.

   b.   How many layers (laminae) does human neocortex have?
         Describe the input to lamina IV and the output from lamina V.

   c.   What is the relationship of columns to laminae? What can be
         said about all the cells within one column?

   d.   What is the current understanding of the relationships among
         sensory, motor, and association areas of cortex? What are the
         sources of input to association cortex?

2. *The occipital lobe*
   a. What are the location and functions of the occipital lobe?

3. *The parietal lobe*
   a. What are the location and functions of the parietal lobe?

4. *The temporal lobe*
   a. Where is the temporal lobe? What are some temporal lobe functions?

5. *The frontal lobe*
   a. What are the location and functions of the frontal lobe? Distinguish between the precentral gyrus and the prefrontal cortex.

   b. What were the results of prefrontal lobotomies?

    c.   What kind of task do monkeys perform poorly after prefrontal lesions?

Methods of investigating how the brain controls behavior
    a.   What was phrenology? What were its half-truths and its weaknesses?

1.   *The stereotaxic instrument*
    a.   What is a stereotaxic instrument and how is it used? What is a stereotaxic atlas?

2.   *Lesions and ablations*
    a.   What are two methods for producing lesions or ablations?

    b.   What is a microtome? For what purpose are histological stains used?

    c.   What problems of interpretation do lesion experiments present?

3.   *Stimulation of and recording from the brain*
    a.   What information have electrical stimulation and recording contributed to our understanding of eating?

4.   *Labeling brain activity*
    a.   Describe two major techniques for labeling brain activity.

5.   *Studies using the natural development of the brain*
    a.   What is the basic conceptual foundation for techniques using genetic lesions, arrested development, and developmental correlations of brain and behavior?

6. *Studies of the structure of living human brains*
   a. Describe the process of computerized axial tomography. What sort of information does it provide?

   b. Describe the process of magnetic resonance imaging. How does it compare with computerized axial tomography? What improved apparatus can form clear images more rapidly than standard MRI?

7. *Measurement of human brain activity*
   a. What are the main advantage and some uses of EEG recording?

   b. What is an evoked potential?

   c. What is the principle behind positron-emission tomography? What are some advantages and disadvantages of this technique?

d. How is regional cerebral blood flow measured? What are two chemicals that appear to increase blood flow to the most active areas of the brain?

POSTTEST

Multiple-Choice Questions

1. Which is true concerning the spinal cord?
    a. Sensory neurons enter on the ventral side; motor neurons exit on the dorsal side.
    b. Cell bodies of sensory neurons lie outside the CNS in the dorsal root ganglia.
    c. Cell bodies of motor neurons lie outside the CNS in the ventral root ganglia.
    d. All of the above are true.

2. The parasympathetic system
    a. is sometimes called the "fight or flight" system.
    b. has a chain of interconnected ganglia along the thoracic and lumbar regions of the spinal cord.
    c. uses norepinephrine as its transmitter to end organs, whereas the sympathetic system uses acetylcholine.
    d. is an energy-conserving system.

3. Concerning the cranial nerves
    a. the first two enter the forebrain, with nuclei in the olfactory bulb and thalamus.
    b. nerves 3-12 enter the medulla.
    c. all have both sensory and motor components.
    d. all have only sensory components.

4. The hindbrain
    a. is composed of the superior and inferior colliculi, the tectum, and the tegmentum.
    b. contains the reticular formation and raphe system.
    c. controls the pituitary gland.
    d. consists of the pons, which is adjacent to the spinal cord; the medulla, which is rostral to the pons; and the cerebellum, ventral to the pons.

5. The cerebellum
   a. contributes to the control of movement and to speed and skill of language and cognition.
   b. is concerned mostly with visual location in space.
   c. is located immediately ventral to the pons.
   d. more than one of the above.

6. The components of the midbrain include
   a. the superior and inferior colliculi in the tectum, involved in sensory processing.
   b. the tegmentum, containing nuclei of the third and fourth cranial nerves, part of the reticular formation, and pathways connecting higher and lower structures.
   c. the substantia nigra, origin of a dopamine-containing pathway that deteriorates in Parkinson's disease.
   d. all of the above.

7. The hypothalamus
   a. is sometimes called the master gland of the body.
   b. is part of the basal ganglia.
   c. is important for motivated behaviors and hormonal control.
   d. is connected only with the brain stem.

8. The basal ganglia
   a. are composed primarily of the caudate nucleus, putamen, and globus pallidus.
   b. control movement directly via axons to the spinal cord.
   c. are primarily concerned with memory.
   d. all of the above.

9. The hippocampus
   a. controls breathing, heart rate, and other vital reflexes.
   b. provides the major control for the pituitary gland.
   c. is part of the basal ganglia.
   d. none of the above.

10. The thalamus contains
   a. the superior and inferior colliculi.
   b. nuclei that project to, and receive axons from, particular areas of cerebral cortex.
   c. nuclei that regulate the pituitary.
   d. nuclei having to do with motivated behaviors, such as eating, drinking, sex, fighting, arousal level, and temperature regulation.

11. Cerebrospinal fluid
    a. is formed by cells lining the four ventricles.
    b. flows from the lateral ventricles to the third and fourth ventricles, and from there either to the central canal of the spinal cord or to the subarachnoid space, where it is reabsorbed into the blood vessels.
    c. cushions the brain and provides buoyancy.
    d. all of the above.

12. The laminae of the cortex
    a. usually consist of only two layers, one of axons and one of cell bodies.
    b. are always the same thickness throughout the brain of a given species, though they may differ across species.
    c. consist of up to six layers, which vary in thickness across the various brain areas.
    d. are present only in humans; other mammals have cells and axons mixed together in the cortex.

13. Which of the following is true of cortical columns?
    a. Columns run parallel to the laminae, across the surface of the cortex.
    b. There are six columns in the human brain, and only one or two in other mammals.
    c. Cells within a column have similar response properties.
    d. The properties of cells within a column change systematically from top to bottom; cells at the top may respond to one stimulus, while those at the bottom respond to a different one.

14. Association areas of the cortex
    a. get all their input from the sensory cortex.
    b. receive input directly from the thalamus, as well as from the sensory cortex.
    c. receive input only from the thalamus.
    d. are areas set aside for a special kind of "associational" information.

15. Which is true of the occipital lobe?
    a. It is located at the posterior end of the cortex and contains primary visual cortex.
    b. It is located at the sides of the brain and is concerned mostly with perception of complex visual patterns.
    c. It is located immediately behind the central sulcus and contains the postcentral gyrus.
    d. It is located at the top of the brain and contributes to the sense of body image.

16. Which is true of the parietal lobe?
    a. It contains the primary receiving area for axons carrying touch information.
    b. It has a somewhat complicated spatial representation of the body on the postcentral gyrus.
    c. Damage to it on one side sometimes produces neglect of the opposite side of the body.
    d. All of the above are true.

17. The temporal lobe
    a. is located immediately in front of the central sulcus.
    b. is involved in some complex aspects of visual processing.
    c. has as its only function the processing of simple auditory information.
    d. none of the above.

18. Damage to the frontal lobe
    a. may cause losses of spontaneity and social inhibitions and difficulties with delayed response tasks.
    b. is still a widely used surgical technique for mental patients because of its remarkable calming and normalizing tendencies without noticeable side effects.
    c. produces drastic impairments in intelligence.
    d. all of the above.

19. A stereotaxic instrument is used for
    a. producing current to make lesions.
    b. producing evoked potentials.
    c. locating small structures deep within the brain.
    d. recording EEGs.

20. The lesion method
    a. requires careful interpretation of behavioral deficits, including multiple kinds of tests.
    b. uses histological techniques to produce lesions.
    c. is flawed because lowering the electrode kills so many neurons that it is impossible to determine whether a behavioral deficit is a result of the electrical lesion or of the extensive damage produced by the electrode on its way to the lesion site.
    d. more than one of the above.

21. Autoradiography
    a. is used primarily to measure blood flow to various brain areas.
    b. uses the principle that atoms with odd atomic weights have inherent rotation that can be altered by a magnetic field.
    c. may use radioactively labeled 2-deoxy-D-glucose to map relative activity levels in the brain.
    d. may use radioactively labeled antibodies to locate an area that has been damaged.

22. Computerized axial tomography
    a. is preferable to other means of detecting abnormalities because it uses no dyes, X rays, or radioactive chemicals.
    b. uses an EEG record to determine regional cerebral blood flow.
    c. uses radioactive elements that emit positrons, which collide with electrons, releasing two gamma rays for each collision; these gamma rays are recorded.
    d. uses dye injected into the blood for contrast, and multiple X rays through the head at different angles; a computer then constructs an image of the brain.

23. An evoked potential
    a. is recorded from an intracellular electrode in a single neuron.
    b. is an electrical response to a sensory stimulus, recorded using an EEG apparatus.
    c. is used to produce a sham lesion.
    d. is the electrical output of the brain in the absence of external sensory stimuli.

Answers to Multiple-Choice Questions

1. b	6. d	11. d	16. d	21. c
2. d	7. c	12. c	17. b	22. d
3. a	8. a	13. c	18. a	23. b
4. b	9. d	14. b	19. c	
5. a	10. b	15. a	20. a	

Diagrams

1. In the following diagram of a cross section through the spinal cord, label the following structures: dorsal, ventral, sensory nerve, dorsal root ganglion, motor nerve, white matter, gray matter, central canal.

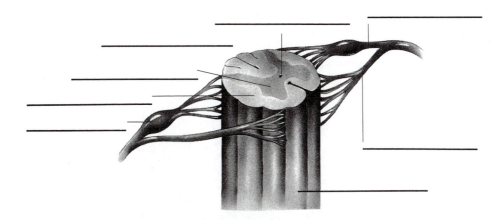

2. In the following diagram of the human cerebral cortex, label the following structures: central sulcus, precentral gyrus, postcentral gyrus, occipital lobe, frontal lobe, parietal lobe, and temporal lobe. Give the functions of each brain area.

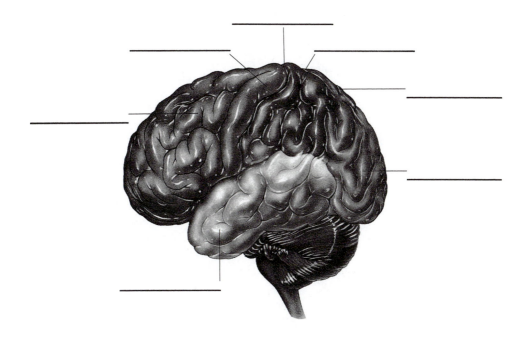

3. In the following diagram of a sagittal section through the human brain, label the following structures: cerebral cortex, parietal lobe, occipital lobe, frontal lobe, cingulate gyrus, corpus callosum, thalamus, hypothalamus, superior and inferior colliculi, midbrain, cerebellum, pons, pituitary gland, tissue dividing the lateral ventricles, medulla, spinal cord, central canal of the spinal cord.

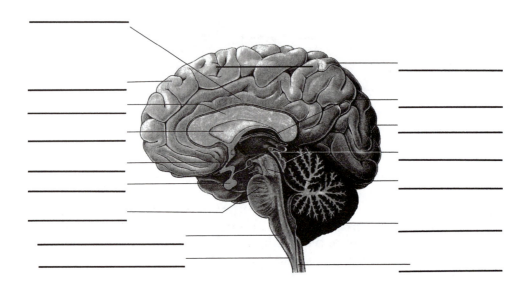

5

DEVELOPMENT AND EVOLUTION
OF THE BRAIN

INTRODUCTION

The central nervous system develops from two long thin lips on the surface of the embryo that merge to form a fluid-filled tube. The forward end of the tube enlarges to become the forebrain, midbrain, and hindbrain; the rest becomes the spinal cord. Cerebrospinal fluid continues to fill the central canal of the spinal cord and four hollow ventricles of the brain. Brain growth consists primarily of the addition of new units, such as the columns of cerebral cortex, but there may be some increase in the size of the units as well.

There are four major stages in the development of neurons: proliferation, migration, differentiation, and myelination. During proliferation, cells lining the ventricles divide. Some of the new cells remain in place and continue dividing, whereas others migrate beyond previous cells to their new destinations. Differentiation includes formation of the axon and dendrites and is influenced by chemical interactions with surrounding neurons. Myelination is the formation, by glial cells, of insulating sheaths around axons, which increase the speed of transmission. The developing brain is more vulnerable than the adult brain to the effects of toxic chemicals, infections, and dietary deficiencies. Experience, such as living in an "enriched" environment or learning bird songs, affects the pattern of dendritic branching.

As the brain grows, axons must travel long distances to reach their appropriate targets. They are guided by concentration gradients of chemicals, such as the protein TOP_{DV}, which guides amphibian retinal neurons to the appropriate part of the tectum. After axons reach the general area of their target, they begin to form synapses with postsynaptic cells. These target cells receive an overabundance of synapses; they gradually strengthen some synapses and reject others. Initially, there are many tentative connections between axons and target cells; later, fewer but stronger attachments develop. As many as half to two-thirds of neurons fail to form any lasting synapses and, as a result, die. The overproduction of neurons and subsequent pruning of unsuccessful connections provide a process of selection of the fittest and enable the nervous system to compensate for variations in body size. The postsynaptic cell's acceptance of synapses from some axons appears to be influenced by the chemical markers on the axon and increased attractiveness due to simultaneous activity by two or more axons.

75

Postsynaptic cells may strengthen connections by releasing growth factors; axons that do not receive enough growth factor degenerate, and their cell bodies may die. Trophic factors typically promote the survival and growth of only certain kinds of neurons; others guide the growth of axons to a particular destination. Pioneer neurons form connections early in development when the brain is relatively small; they serve as a guide to later developing neurons that have a longer distance to traverse. Many of these pioneer neurons, including the subplate neurons just beneath the developing cerebral cortex, survive only long enough to mark the path for thalamic and cortical axons to reach their targets.

It is difficult to infer the evolution of brain or behavior. However, if a given structure is organized similarly in all mammals, we can infer that that genes regulating the formation of that structure were inherited from a common ancester. Among mammals the forebrain forms a larger proportion of the brain than in fish, amphibians, and reptiles. Furthermore, the size of a sensory area of the brain corresponds roughly to the extent to which a species uses that sense. Primates have greater development of the cerebral cortex than other mammals; this resulted primarily from addition of new areas, rather than expansion of old areas. Both absolute brain size and brain-to-body ratio are sometimes correlated with measures of intelligence, both across species and among humans. However, it is difficult to measure comparative intelligence across species, and we need much more information on the contribution of specific neurons in various brain areas to specific behavioral abilities before we can understand the relationship of brain size to intelligence.

KEY TERMS AND CONCEPTS

Development of the brain
1. Growth and differentiation of the vertebrate brain
   Neural tube
   Hindbrain
   Midbrain
   Forebrain
   Central canal of spinal cord
   Ventricles
   Cerebrospinal fluid (CSF)
   Growth and development of neurons
      Addition of new units
      Expansion of old units
      Proliferation
      Migration
      Differentiation
      Myelination

        Vulnerability of the developing brain
                Infections
                        Syphilis
                        Rubella
                Cretinism
                        Deficiency of iodine and thyroid hormones
                Fetal alcohol syndrome
                        Short, less branched dendrites
        Modification by experience
                Enriched environment
                        More glia
                        Wider dendritic branches
                Bird song learning
                        Dendritic spines

2.   Pathfinding by axons
        Chemical pathfinding by axons
                Axons to extra leg of salamander
                Optic tract axons to tectum of newts and fish
                TOP_{DV}
        Competition among axons
                Overproduction of neurons
                Elimination of synapses
                Massive cell death
                Survival of the fittest
                Compensation for unpredictable size
                Mechanisms determining acceptance
                        Chemical markers on axons
                        Simultaneous activity of axons
                                Lateral geniculate
        Chemical mechanisms of neuron death and neuron survival
                Nerve growth factor
                Trophic factors
                        Survival of dopamine neurons
                        Thalamic axons to layer 4 of cortex

3.   Competition among axons as a general principle
        Neural Darwinism
        Pioneer neurons
                Subplate cells

Evolution of the brain and its capacities
1.   Difficulties of inferring evolution of brain or behavior
        Similarity of primary visual cortex among mammals
        Dissimilarities of other cortical areas

2. Human brains and other brains
   Correlation of use with size of brain area
   Folding of cerebral cortex
   Addition of new areas
   Size of prefrontal cortex

3. Brain size and intelligence
   Brain size, body size, and intelligence across species
       Absolute brain size
       Brain-to-body ratio
   Problems of measuring animal intelligence
       Concept of oddity
   Doubts about the value of brain-to-body ratio
   Variations in brain size and intelligence among humans
   Biological factors influencing brain size
   Correlations between brain size and intelligence
       MRI
   Possible relationship to race or ethnic differences

SHORT-ANSWER QUESTIONS

Development of the brain
1. *Growth and differentiation of the vertebrate brain*
   a. Describe the formation of the central nervous system in the
       embryo. What happens to the fluid-filled cavity?

   b. What are the three main divisions of the brain?

c. What technical development by LaMantia and Purves increased our understanding of brain development? What was their major finding?

d. What are the four major stages in the development of neurons? Describe the processes in each.

e. What is cretinism? What causes it?

f. Describe fetal alcohol syndrome. How are dendrites affected? How much alcohol is necessary to produce the syndrome?

g. Describe the effects of environmental "enrichment."

h. What physiological process appears to be correlated with song learning in mynah birds?

2. *Pathfinding by axons*
    a. What did Weiss observe in his experiments on salamanders' extra limbs? What principle did he conclude directed the innervation of the extra limb? Is this principle still believed to be correct?

    b. What did Sperry observe when he damaged the optic nerve of newts? What happened when he rotated the eye by 180 degrees? How did the newt with the rotated eye see the world?

    c. What conclusion did these results suggest?

d. What is TOP$_{DV}$? What is its role in directing retinal axons to the tectum?

e. What happened when retinal tissue of fetal rats was transplanted into the interior of the brain?

f. Describe the pattern of goldfish retinal connections when half the tectum was destroyed. when half the retina was destroyed. What does this suggest about the precision of connections of axons with target cells?

g. What happens to axons that form active synapses? What happens to axons that do not form active synapses?

h. What two factors might lead a postsynaptic cell to accept certain synapses but not others? How does a lateral geniculate neuron "know" which axons originated near one another in the retina?

i.   What is the rationale for the overproduction and massive death of neurons early in development?

j.   Who discovered nerve growth factor? What happens if a neuron in the sympathetic nervous system does not receive enough nerve growth factor?

k.   What are the roles of some other trophic factors?

3.   *Competition among axons as a general principle of neural functioning*
     a.   Describe the principle of neural Darwinism. How does this relate to the initial overproduction and subsequent death of large numbers of neurons?

b. How does neural Darwinism differ from Darwinian evolution of species?

c. What is the point of having subplate cells if they do not survive very long?

Evolution of the brain and its capacities
1. *Difficulties of inferring evolution of brain or behavior*
    a. What inferences about evolution of the visual system can we draw from the similarity of the primary visual cortex across mammalian species? What does the dissimilarity of supplementary visual areas imply?

2. *Human brains and other brains*
    a. Describe some of the similarities and differences among vertebrate brains.

b.   What can we infer about the amount of folding of the cerebral cortex?

c.   What are several distinctive features of the human brain?

3.   *Brain size and intelligence*
   a.   What is the best mathematical predictor of the size of the brain? Is absolute brain size or brain-to-body ratio more highly correlated with informal estimates of intelligence?

   b.   What can we say about monkeys' and rats' relative abilities to acquire the concept of oddity? What intellectual skills, if any, have been demonstrated in primates but not in adequately tested lower animals?

c. Why is the relationship between body and brain size within a species a weak one?

d. Describe the recent evidence of a relationship between brain size and intelligence.

e. What additional information do we need before we can understand the relationship between brain structures and intelligence?

POSTTEST

Multiple-Choice Questions

1. The neural tube
   a. arises from a pair of long thin lips that merge around a fluid-filled cavity.
   b. develops into the spinal cord; the brain arises from a separate structure.
   c. eventually merges to form a solid structure, squeezing out the primitive cerebrospinal fluid.
   d. none of the above.

2. As the brain grows
   a. the number of columns stays the same, but the size of each column increases.
   b. the columns that were characteristic of the infant brain merge to form one continuous functional unit in the adult.
   c. the number of columns increases considerably, but the average size of columns increases only a little.
   d. the size of each column increases considerably, but the number of columns actually decreases.

3. The cerebral cortex develops
   a. from cells whose characteristics are fully programmed genetically.
   b. from cells dividing on the outermost layer of the brain.
   c. from the outside in, with new cells remaining nearer their site of formation in the ventricles.
   d. from the inside out, with new cells migrating beyond previous cells.

4. Cretinism
   a. is caused by a deficiency of iodine during adulthood.
   b. is caused by a deficiency of iodine in a fetus or infant.
   c. is apparent immediately at birth.
   d. results directly from excessively high levels of thyroid hormones during infancy.

5. Fetal alcohol syndrome
   a. results in decreased alertness, hyperactivity, varying degrees of mental retardation, motor problems, heart defects, and facial abnormalities.
   b. is observed only in children whose mothers drank very large quantities of alcohol throughout pregnancy.
   c. results in cretinism.
   d. all of the above.

6. Environmental enrichment produces
   a. no changes in the structure of neurons, only changes in their function.
   b. a smaller number of dendritic spines.
   c. a larger number of glial cells.
   d. a larger number of neurons.

7. During their first year, mynah birds
    a. have decreasing numbers of dendritic spines in the song control areas of the brain.
    b. have an increase in size of the surviving dendritic spines.
    c. learn many songs, but, by the end of the year, lose the ability to learn additional songs.
    d. all of the above.

8. When Paul Weiss grafted an extra leg onto a salamander
    a. the extra leg received no neurons and therefore could not move.
    b. the extra leg moved in the opposite direction from the normal adjacent leg.
    c. the extra leg moved in synchrony with the normal adjacent leg.
    d. the leg degenerated because the immune system rejected it.

9. Sperry's work with the eyes of newts and goldfish led him to conclude that
    a. neurons attach to postsynaptic cells randomly, and the postsynaptic cell confers specificity of function.
    b. axons follow a chemical trail that places them in the general vicinity of their target.
    c. innervation in the sensory system is guided by specific genetic information, whereas that in the motor system is random.
    d. neurons follow specific genetic information that directs each of them to precisely the right postsynaptic cell.

10. TOP_{DV}
    a. is a trophic factor necessary for the survival of neurons of the sympathetic nervous system.
    b. is a protein that is more concentrated neurons of the dorsal retina and the ventral tectum than in the ventral retina and dorsal tectum.
    c. is a protein that guides axons to the developing legs of newts.
    d. is a protein that causes a group of neurons that possess it to fire together, thereby increasing their chance of survival.

11. If the caudal half of the goldfish tectum is removed and the optic nerve is cut, the retinal axons that would have made contact with the removed part
    a. form synapses with the most caudal part of the remaining tectum.
    b. die, because their target is missing.
    c. make random connections throughout the remaining tectum, because their chemical "map" is missing.
    d. grow back toward the retina and make synapses with other retinal neurons.

12. Massive cell death early in development
    a. is a normal result of unsuccessful competition for synapses and growth factors.
    b. occurs only when the sensory environment has been highly restricted or when the fetus has been exposed to toxins.
    c. occurs as a result of genetic mistakes, which fail to direct the cells to their genetically programmed target. As a result the neurons wander aimlessly until they die.
    d. would be so maladaptive that it hardly ever occurs.

13. Which of the following is true?
    a. A postsynaptic cell is more likely to form synapses with groups of axons whose activity is uncorrelated with one another rather than with those that are simultaneously active, because that provides the postsynaptic cell with a greater range of information.
    b. If a postsynaptic cell finds a synapse unacceptable, it sends out a rejection chemical that causes the axon to degenerate.
    c. Excess neurons enable the nervous system to compensate for variations in body size.
    d. All of the above are true.

14. Nerve growth factor
    a. is important for the health of all neurons throughout life.
    b. is important for the initial survival of all neurons but becomes less important after synapses are formed.
    c. is important for the survival of motor, but not sensory, neurons.
    d. is important for the survival and growth of sympathetic neurons.

15. Lamina 4 of the cerebral cortex
    a. produces less growth factor than do laminae 6 and 5; this results in thalamic axons stopping there.
    b. produces more growth factor than do laminae 6 and 5; this attracts more thalamic axons.
    c. produces a factor that repels incoming axons from the cerebral cortex, so that synaptic sites will be available for the slower maturing thalamic cells.
    d. is the site of motor neuron cell bodies.

16. Neural Darwinism
    a. was formulated by Roger Sperry.
    b. proposes that synapses form somewhat randomly at first; those that work best are kept, while the others degenerate.
    c. has recently been shown to be false.
    d. all of the above.

17. Subplate cells
    a. surround the thalamus and supply nerve growth factor to thalamic cells as their axons journey to the cortex.
    b. form a permanent docking area beneath the cortex where thalamic and cortical cells meet.
    c. serve as pioneer neurons, surviving only briefly but laying down paths to be used by later-developing permanent neurons.
    d. form the outermost layer of the cortex after all of the thalamic cells have arrived.

Answers to Multiple-Choice Questions

1. a	6. c	10. b	14. d
2. c	7. d	11. a	15. a
3. d	8. c	12. a	16. b
4. b	9. b	13. c	17. c
5. a			

6

VISION

INTRODUCTION

Sensory systems, including vision, are concerned with reception (absorption of physical energy) and transduction of that energy into neural activity that encodes some aspect of the stimulus. The structure of each kind of sensory receptor allows it to be stimulated maximally by one kind of energy, and little or not at all by other forms of energy. The brain interprets any information sent by nerves that synapse with those receptors as being about that form of energy. This principle was described by Müller as the law of specific nerve energies. This principle has been updated with three additional stipulations: (1) increases and decreases from a spontaneous rate of firing may signal different stimuli; (2) the rhythm of impulses may code certain kinds of sensory information; and (3) perception is determined by activity of the whole system.

Light is focused by the cornea and lens onto the retina, which contains two kinds of receptors. Cones are most densely packed in the fovea, an area in the center of the retina with the most acute (detailed) vision. This acuity is largely the result of the small number of cones that synapse with each bipolar cell. Rods are located more peripherally in the retina than are cones and are more sensitive to low levels of light. Furthermore, each bipolar receives input from a large number of rods. This improves sensitivity to dim light but sacrifices acuity.

All photopigments contain 11-cis-retinal bound to one of several opsins. Light converts 11-cis-retinal to all-trans-retinal, triggering a change in the opsin, which in turn activates second-messenger molecules. This results in the closing of ion channels, which hyperpolarizes the receptor. In the dark the receptor steadily discharges an inhibitory transmitter; light decreases the output of that transmitter.

Cones mediate color vision because three different photopigments are found in three types of cones. Each photopigment is maximally sensitive to one wavelength of light but responds less readily to other wavelengths. Thus, each wavelength produces a certain ratio of responses from the three receptors; the ratio remains essentially constant regardless of brightness. Rods, in contrast to cones, contain only one photopigment and therefore do not contribute directly to our perception of colors. Processing of color vision beyond the receptor level depends on an opponent-process mechanism, in which a given cell responds to one color with increased firing and to another color with a decrease below its spontaneous rate of firing.

Visual input is processed neurally in order to provide an organized, useful representation of the environment. A visual receptor is able not only to stimulate its own bipolar(s) but also to inhibit activity in neighboring bipolars. It accomplishes this feat through the cooperation of horizontal cells, which receive input from a number of receptors and synapse with a number of bipolars. Electrical activity can flow in all directions in horizontal cells. The advantage of this arrangement is that borders are enhanced at the expense of redundant input. The process is called lateral inhibition.

A receptive field of a neuron in the visual system is that set of receptors in the retina in which the presence or absence of light affects its firing rate. Most receptive fields contain both excitatory and inhibitory regions. The receptive fields of bipolar, ganglion, and geniculate cells are concentric circles. For some cells light in the center is excitatory, and for other cells it is inhibitory; light in the surround has the opposite effect. Cells in the visual cortex (occipital lobe) have bar shaped receptive fields as a result of summing the receptive fields of their lateral geniculate cell inputs.

Ganglion cells have been divided into two major types. X cells are relatively small cells, located in or near the fovea, that respond in a sustained manner to a sustained stimulus. Y cells are larger, are spread evenly across the retina, and respond transiently even to sustained stimuli. A smaller group of cells, W cells, respond weakly to light and are poorly understood.

At the lateral geniculate nucleus of the thalamus, X cells synapse with parvocellular (small) neurons, and both X and Y cells synapse with magnocellular (large) neurons. Parvocellular neurons are well suited to analyze stationary stimuli because they have small receptive fields and respond in a sustained manner. They also discriminate colors. Magnocellular neurons are color blind, respond quickly but briefly to a sustained stimulus, and are well suited to detect movement.

Most of the input from the lateral geniculate goes to the primary visual cortex (area V1), which in turn projects to secondary visual cortex (area V2), along with some input directly from the thalamus. From area V2, information branches out to areas V3, V4, and V5, and ultimately to twenty or more areas that receive visual input. At the cortex, the parvocellular and magnocellular systems split into three pathways. One pathway processes shape information from the parvocellular system. Another processes movement information from the magnocellular system. The third pathway processes brightness input from the magnocellular system and color information from the parvocellular system.

David Hubel and Torsten Wiesel received the Nobel Prize for their pioneering work on feature detectors in the visual cortex. They distinguished three categories of neurons: simple, complex, and hypercomplex. Simple cells respond maximally to a bar oriented in a particular direction and in a particular location on the retina. Excitatory and inhibitory areas may be mapped with small spots of light. Complex cells, on the other hand, have larger receptive fields, respond to correctly oriented bars located anywhere within the field, and do not respond to small spots of light. Most complex cells respond preferentially to movement in one direction. Hypercomplex cells are like complex cells, except for an area of strong inhibition at one end of the field. Cortical cells with similar properties are grouped in columns perpendicular to the surface. Cells within a column have overlapping receptive fields and respond to similar features. Adjacent columns analyze slightly different features.

Additional processing of shape information is accomplished by area V3 of the magnocellular system, which identifies the overall shape or outline of an object, and by inferior temporal cortex, which responds preferentially to highly complex shapes such as hands or faces. Damage to the pattern recognition areas results in visual agnosia, the inability to recognize visual objects. Some people have difficulty identifying almost all objects; others experience agnosia for only one or a few classes of stimuli. Although each cell in inferior temporal cortex is more responsive to some stimuli than to others, it does respond fairly strongly to a range of similar objects. Therefore, no one cell is the only detector for a given object.

Area V4 is especially important for color perception. Damage to this area results in either color blindness or loss of color constancy, which is the ability to recognize the color of an object despite changes in lighting. Area V4 receives color input from the parvocellular system and brightness information from the magnocellular system. It also contributes to visual attention.

Some cells in the magnocellular system are specialized for depth perception. They are sensitive to the amount of discrepancy between the images from the two eyes. Another branch of the magnocellular system detects motion. It projects to area V5 (middle temporal cortex) and an adjacent area (medial superior temporal cortex). Some neurons in these areas respond preferentially to different speeds and directions of movement, without analyzing the object that is moving. Others prefer certain kinds of stimuli, such as small moving light-dark borders, or expanding, contracting, or rotating large scenes. These cells allow us to perceive the motion of an object against a stationary field. There is no single area of the brain that puts together all the information about a given object. One possible mechanism for connecting responses in many brain areas is 40 cycle-per-second oscillations that are produced in synchrony with one another.

Cells in the mammalian visual cortex are endowed at the individual's birth with certain adultlike characteristics. However, normal sensory experience is necessary to develop these characteristics fully and to prevent them from degenerating. If only one eye is deprived of vision during an early sensitive period, the brain becomes unresponsive to that eye. Input from the active eye suppresses the early connections made by the inactive eye. It is likely that axons from the active eye compete successfully for nerve growth factor provided by the postsynaptic cells. If both eyes are deprived, cortical cells remain at least somewhat responsive to both. Later visual experience does not restore responsiveness to the previously inactive eye, unless the previously active eye is covered for a prolonged time. Other aspects of vision that require early experience for proper development are stereoscopic depth perception, ability to see lines of a given direction, and motion perception.

KEY TERMS AND CONCEPTS

Visual coding and the retinal receptors
1. Reception, transduction and coding
    Generator potential
    Law of specific nerve energies
    Spontaneous rate of firing
    Rhythm of impulses

2. The eye and its connections to the brain
    Cornea
    Pupil
    Lens
    Retina
    Fovea
    Visual streak
    Receptors
        Rods
        Cones
    Bipolar neurons
    Ganglion cells
    Optic nerve
        Blind spot

3. Visual receptors: rods and cones
    Chemical basis for receptor excitation
        Photopigments
        11-cis-retinal
        All-trans-retinal
        Opsin
    Transduction
    Hyperpolarization

4. Color vision
    Trichromatic (Young-Helmholtz) theory
        Psychophysical color matching

93

Opponent-process (Hering) theory
    Negative afterimage
Color blindness: sex linked

Neural basis of visual perception

1. An overview of the mammalian visual system
Retina
    Receptors
    Horizontal cells
    Bipolar cells
    Amacrine cells
    Ganglion cells
Lateral geniculate nucleus
Cerebral cortex

2. Mechanisms of processing in the visual system
Receptive fields
Lateral inhibition
    Horizontal cells
    Bipolar cells
How receptive fields are built
    Concentric circles in retina and lateral geniculate
    Bars and edges in cortex

3. Parallel pathways in the visual system
Parallel pathways in retina and lateral geniculate
    X cells: small, in fovea, sustained response
    Y cells: large, even distribution, brief response
    W cells: weak response
    Parvocellular lateral geniculate cells
        Input from X cells
        Color discrimination
        Good acuity
    Magnocellular lateral geniculate cells
        Input from X and Y cells
        Color blind
        Detect movement
Parallel pathways in the cerebral cortex
    Primary visual cortex, striate cortex (V1)
    Secondary visual cortex (V2)
    V3, V4, V5
    Twenty or more brain areas receiving visual input
    Three pathways
        Details of shape (parvocellular)
        Movement (magnocellular)
        Brightness (magnocellular) and color (parvocellular)

Cerebral cortex: The shape pathway
    Hubel and Wiesel
    Feature detectors
    Binocular receptive fields
    Simple cells (V1)
        Bar shaped receptive field
        Receptive field mapped by a point of light
    Complex cells (V1 and V2)
        Larger receptive fields
        No response to point of light
        Response to moving bar of light
    Hypercomplex cells
        Strong inhibitory area at one end of bar-shaped receptive
            field
    Columnar organization of the visual cortex
        Columns perpendicular to surface
        Similar response properties within a column
    Feature detectors and human vision
    Shape analysis beyond the primary and secondary visual cortices
        Inferior temporal cortex
            Advanced pattern analysis
            Shape constancy
    Disorders of object recognition
        Visual agnosia
            Prosopagnosia
            Distinctive pattern across a population of neurons
Cerebral cortex: The color pathway
    Area V4
    Color constancy
    Input from parvocellular (color) and magnocellular (brightness)
        pathways
    Visual attention
Cerebral cortex: The motion and depth pathways
    Stereoscopic depth perception
        Magnocellular pathway
    Structures important for motion perception
        Area V5 (middle temporal cortex, MT)
        Medial superior temporal cortex (MST)
    Motion blindness
    Is motion perception color blind?
Cerebral cortex: Communication among the pathways
    40 cycle-per-second oscillations

4. Development of the visual system
    Infant vision
    Development of binocular interaction

Effects of early lack of stimulation of one eye
    Sensitive, or critical, period
Effects of early lack of stimulation of both eyes
Restoration of response after early deprivation of vision
    Lazy eye, or amblyopia ex anopsia
Deprivation of the simultaneous use of both eyes
    Stereoscopic depth perception
    Retinal disparity
    Strabismus
    Synchronous messages
    Nerve growth factor
Development of pattern perception
    Effects of early total visual deprivation
        Difficulty identifying objects visually
    Effects of early exposure to a limited array of patterns
    Astigmatism
Development of other aspects of vision
    Stroboscopic illumination
        Motion blindness
    Color vision unaffected by color restriction
Blind spots and blindsight
    Superior colliculus
Seeing while the eye grows

SHORT-ANSWER QUESTIONS

Visual coding and the retinal receptors
1. *Reception, transduction and coding*
    a.   Distinguish between reception, transduction, and coding.

    b.   What is a generator potential?

c. Does the inverted visual image pose a problem for the visual system?

d. State the law of specific nerve energies. Who formulated it?

e. How does this law apply to neurons with spontaneous firing rates?

f. What two additional modifications of this principle seem necessary in light of current knowledge?

2. *The eye and its connections to the brain*
   a. What is the fovea? How did it get its name?

b. How have many bird species solved the problem of getting detailed information in two different directions?

c. Trace the path of visual information from a receptor to the optic nerve. What is the blind spot?

3. *Visual receptors: rods and cones*
    a. Compare peripheral and foveal vision with regard to acuity, sensitivity to dim light, and color vision.

    b. What is the specific role of light in the initiation of a response in a receptor?

    c. What is the relationship of 11-cis-retinal to all-trans-retinal?

d. What is an opsin? What is its role in a photopigment?

e. What kind of electrical response is produced in the receptor, and how does this affect the bipolars with which it synapses?

4. *Color vision*
   a. Why does the presence of cones in the retina of a given species not guarantee color vision? Why does color vision necessarily depend on the pattern of responses of a number of different neurons?

   b. How did Young and Helmholtz propose to account for color vision? On what kind of data was their theory based?

c.   What kind of theory did Hering propose? What observations supported his theory?

d.   What is the current relationship between the three-receptor and the opponent-process theories?

e.   What is the genetic basis for the most common form of color blindness? Why are more males than females color blind?

Neural basis of visual perception
1.   *An overview of the mammalian visual system*
     a.   Draw a diagram showing the relationship among the rods and cones, the bipolar and horizontal cells, and the ganglion and amacrine cells.

b. Axons of which kind of cell form the optic nerve? What is the name of the site where the right and left optic nerves meet? What percentage of axons cross to the opposite side of the brain in humans? in species with eyes far to the sides of their heads?

c. Where do most axons in the optic nerve synapse? Where do some other optic nerve axons synapse?

d. What is the destination of axons from the lateral geniculate nucleus?

2. *Mechanisms of processing in the visual system*
    a. What is the definition of the receptive field of a neuron in the visual system?

b.   What is the advantage of processing sensory information as opposed to transmitting it "accurately" to the brain?

c.   What is lateral inhibition? How does it enhance contrast?

d.   How is lateral inhibition accomplished in the vertebrate retina?

e.   If several bipolar cells provide input to a certain ganglion cell, what can be said about the location of their receptive fields?

f.   How do receptive fields of lateral geniculate cells differ from those of visual cortical cells?

g. Describe the set of synaptic connections that might produce a bar-shaped receptive field characteristic of cortical cells.

3. *Parallel pathways in the visual system*
    a. Describe the responses of X and Y ganglion cells.

    b. What are parvocellular lateral geniculate neurons? Which ganglion cells provide input to parvocellular neurons?

    c. What are magnocellular lateral geniculate neurons? Which ganglion cells provide input to magnocellular neurons?

    d. Contrast the responses of parvocellular and magnocellular neurons.

e.   Trace the routes of visual information in the cortex.

f.   What are the two sources of input to area V2? How much of the brain receives visual input?

g.   What type of information does each of the three main parallel visual pathways process?

4.   *Cerebral cortex: The shape pathway*
   a.   For what accomplishment did David Hubel and Torsten Wiesel share the Nobel Prize? What is a "feature detector?"

   b.   Describe the receptive fields of simple cells.

c.   What are two differences between responses of simple and complex visual cortical cells?

d.   Describe the receptive field of a hypercomplex cell?

e.   What can be said about the receptive fields of neurons lying above and below one another in the visual cortex? about neurons lying next to one another?

f.   Which two areas, beyond the primary and secondary visual cortices, are important for shape analysis? What is the major contribution of each?

g.   Describe the symptoms of visual agnosia. What is prosopagnosia?

5. *Cerebral cortex: The color pathway*
   a. Describe the receptive fields of neurons in area V4. What is the special function of area V4?

   b. What might the magnocellular pathway, which does not analyze color information directly, contribute to color constancy?

6. *Cerebral cortex: The motion and depth pathways*
   a. What type of neurons are specialized for stereoscopic depth perception? To what aspect of the visual stimulus are they highly sensitive?

   b. Which two areas of the cortex are specialized for motion perception? How "picky" are cells in these areas to the specific characteristics of the stimulus that is moving?

   c. Describe the response characteristics of some cells in area V5.

d. Describe the preferred stimuli for some cells in area MST. What contribution to perception would these cells provide?

e. What is the role of cells in the ventral part of MST?

f. Describe the symptoms of motion blindness.

7. *Cerebral cortex: Communication among the pathways*
    a. Summarize the main ideas of visual information processing?

    b. What is one possible means of connecting all aspects of visual information processing into a unified perception?

Development of the visual system
1. *Infant vision*
    a. What is the advantage of having the eyes approach their full adult size sooner than the rest of the body?

    b. Describe the visual abilities of young infants. Do they see better in the periphery or in the center of their visual field?

    c. How easy is it for infants to shift their attention to other visual stimuli?

2. *Development of binocular interaction*
    a. What is a sensitive or critical period?

    b. What is the effect of depriving only one eye of pattern vision during the critical period? What happens if both eyes are closed during that period?

c.   For what human condition does this principle have relevance? What is the usual treatment for this condition? Why is it important to begin treatment as early as possible?

d.   Define retinal disparity. How does the brain use this information to produce stereoscopic depth perception?

e.   What is the effect of allowing a kitten to use only one eye at a time during the sensitive period for visual development?

f.   What human disorder is analogous to the situation in the previous question? Does surgical correction in adulthood improve depth perception in people with this disorder?

g.   What chemical may promote survival of synapses from the most active eye?

3. *Development of pattern perception*
    a. Describe the responses to light of visual cortical cells in kittens whose eyes had just been opened. How were they similar to, or different from, the responses of normal adult cortical cells?

    b. What happens to the response characteristics of visual cortical cells in a kitten exposed to only vertical or horizontal lines early in life?

    c. Define astigmatism. What happens if a child has severe, uncorrected astigmatism during the first few years of life?

4. *Development of other aspects of vision*
    a. What was the result of raising kittens in an environment illuminated only by a strobe light?

b. What happens to color vision if a monkey can see only red light for the first three months of life?

POSTTEST

Multiple-Choice Questions

1. The one-to-one correspondence between some aspect of the physical stimulus and some aspect of the nervous system activity is known as
   a. reception
   b. transduction
   c. coding
   d. a generator potential

2. The law of specific nerve energies
   a. implies that if the visual receptors were connected to the auditory nerve, and the auditory receptors were connected to the optic nerve, we would "see" sounds and "hear" lights.
   b. states that the kind of message a nerve carries depends only on the kind of stimulus that initiated it; that is, light can give rise only to visual messages, and so on.
   c. is true as it was originally stated; therefore, both increases and decreases in firing rates of cells with spontaneous firing rates must signal the same thing.
   d. is no longer thought to be true, and is now only of historical interest.

3. The fovea
   a. is completely blind because axons from ganglion cells exit from the retina there.
   b. covers approximately half the retina.
   c. contains no rods and is bypassed by most blood vessels and axons of more distant ganglion cells.
   d. is color blind because it contains no cones but has good sensitivity to dim light.

4. Which of the following is true?
   a. Cones are more sensitive to dim light than are rods.
   b. Cones mediate more detailed vision because relatively few cones synapse with each bipolar.
   c. Cones mediate more detailed vision because of their shape.
   d. Cones are situated peripherally in the retina, rods more centrally, though there is some overlap.

5. A photopigment molecule absorbs a photon of light whose energy converts
   a. all-trans-retinal to 11-cis-retinal. Somehow this leads to hyperpolarization of the receptor.
   b. 11-cis-retinal to all-trans-retinal. Somehow this leads to hyperpolarization of the receptor.
   c. 11-cis-retinal to all-trans-retinal. Somehow this leads to depolarization of the receptor.
   d. opsin to all-trans-retinal. Somehow this leads to depolarization of the receptor.

6. The opponent-process theory
   a. is now thought to describe color processing by neurons after the receptor level, whereas the Young-Helmholtz theory describes activity at the receptor level.
   b. is now thought to describe color processing at the receptor level, whereas the Young-Helmholtz theory describes processing at higher levels.
   c. states that each receptor is sensitive only to a narrow band of wavelengths of light and that bands of different receptor groups do not overlap.
   d. is true only for rods, not cones.

7. The most common form of colorblindness
   a. is more common in women than in in men.
   b. has been well known since the earliest civilizations.
   c. is characterized by difficulty distinguishing blue from yellow.
   d. is characterized by difficulty distinguishing red from green.

8. Which of the following best describes the route of visual information in the retina?
   a. receptor-->bipolar cell-->ganglion cell
   b. receptor-->ganglion cell-->bipolar cell
   c. receptor-->ganglion cell-->amacrine cell
   d. receptor-->horizontal cell-->amacrine cell

9. Which of the following is true concerning receptive fields?
    a. They are always defined as an area surrounding "their" neuron; the receptive field for a simple cortical cell is itself in the cortex.
    b. The presence of both excitatory and inhibitory areas in the same receptive field is maladaptive and is a holdover from an earlier, inefficient way of processing information.
    c. Receptive fields of simple cortical cells are circular.
    d. For mammalian ganglion cells, they are generally circular, with the center being either excitatory or inhibitory and the surround being the opposite.

10. Lateral inhibition
    a. increases sensitivity to dim light.
    b. ordinarily decreases contrast at borders.
    c. ordinarily heightens contrast at borders.
    d. interferes with processing of color information.

11. Horizontal cells
    a. send axons out of the retina through the blind spot.
    b. help to enhance contrast at borders by inhibiting neighboring bipolar cells.
    c. are located behind the receptors so that they are out of the way of incoming light bound for receptors.
    d. all of the above.

12. X cells
    a. are located primarily in the periphery of the retina.
    b. are highly sensitive to both detail and color.
    c. are among the largest ganglion cells in the retina.
    d. respond only weakly to visual stimuli.

13. Parvocellular lateral geniculate neurons
    a. receive input from X cells and discriminate colors and fine details.
    b. receive input from W cells and detect movement.
    c. receive input from Y cells and are color blind.
    d. receive input from X, Y, and W cells and contribute to larger shape patterns, depth, movement and color discrimination.

14. The parvocellular and magnocellular systems
    a. merge in area V1, and remain one system for subsequent analysis.
    b. remain as two systems throughout visual processing.
    c. divide into three systems, with most of the parvocellular system continuing to analyze details of shape, most of the magnocellular system analyzing movement, and the third system containing parvocellular cells that analyze color and magnocellular cells that analyze brightness.
    d. divide into many parallel pathways, each analyzing a different color, direction of movement, or shape.

15. Simple cells in the visual cortex
    a. respond maximally to bars of light oriented in one direction but not to bars of light oriented in another direction.
    b. respond to "correctly" oriented bars of light only when they are in the "correct" part of the retina.
    c. were first described by Hubel and Wiesel.
    d. all of the above.

16. Simple and complex cells differ in that
    a. the receptive field of a complex cell cannot be mapped into fixed excitatory and inhibitory zones.
    b. the receptive field of a simple cell is larger than that of a complex cell.
    c. a simple cell is practically unaffected by small spots of light.
    d. all of the above.

17. Simple and complex cells are similar in that
    a. most of them receive binocular input.
    b. most respond maximally to bars of light or dark oriented in a particular direction.
    c. both may be found in the striate cortex.
    d. all of the above.

18. Hypercomplex cells
    a. have extremely small receptive fields.
    b. are similar to complex cells except that there is a strong inhibitory area at one end of the receptive field.
    c. respond only to very complex stimuli, such as faces.
    d. respond very well to small spots of light.

19. Neurons along the track of an electrode inserted perpendicular to the surface of visual cortex
    a. have response characteristics that vary from the top to the bottom.
    b. have random response characteristics.
    c. have certain response characteristics in common.
    d. cannot have their responses recorded, since the electrode damages them severely.

20. Area V3
    a. is part of the magnocelllular system.
    b. is important for identification of the overall shape of an object.
    c. has receptive fields that are larger and more complex than in areas V1 and V2.
    d. all of the above.

21. The inferior temporal cortex
    a. has receptive fields that always include the fovea.
    b. is concerned with advanced pattern analysis and complex shapes.
    c. may provide our sense of shape constancy.
    d. all of the above.

22. A person with visual agnosia
    a. may have lost recognition only for a few kinds of stimuli, such as faces, as in prosopagnosia.
    b. has lost the ability to read.
    c. is blind.
    d. results from damage to primary visual cortex.

23. Area V4
    a. is especially important for face recognition.
    b. is especially important for color constancy.
    c. is especially important for shape constancy.
    d. receives input only from the parvocellular system.

24. Occipital area V5 (MT, middle temporal cortex) and MST (medial superior temporal cortex)
    a. analyze complex shapes.
    b. analyze colors.
    c. analyze speed and direction of movement.
    d. analyze stereoscopic depth cues.

25. Cells in MST that respond to expansion, contraction, or rotation of a large visual scene
    a. probably help to record the movement of the head with respect to the world.
    b. probably help to keep track of a single object.
    c. are very particular about the specific objects in their receptive field.
    d. receive input primarily from the parvocellular system.

26. Various aspects of an object may be "put together" by
    a. hypercomplex cells
    b. area V5
    c. inferotemporal cortex
    d. 40 cycle-per-second oscillations by neurons stimulated by the same object.

27. Human infants
    a. are unable to see patterns for at least several weeks.
    b. see better in their central field of vision because their fovea develops before the periphery of the retina.
    c. have trouble shifting their attention before about 6 months of age.
    d. all of the above.

28. If a kitten's eyelid is sutured shut for the first 6 weeks of life, and the sutures are then removed, the kitten
    a. is totally blind in the inactive eye only if the other eye had normal visual input.
    b. is totally blind in the inactive eye regardless of the other eye's visual experience.
    c. is able to see horizontal and vertical lines, but not diagonal lines or curves.
    d. sees normally out of the eye, since all of its connections were formed before birth.

29. Children with lazy eye (amblyopia ex anopsia)
    a. should have the active eye covered continuously until adulthood.
    b. should have the active eye covered as early as possible, but only until the lazy eye becomes functional.
    c. should have the active eye covered only after they have reached normal adult size, in order to avoid reorganization of connections.
    d. should not be treated at all, since they will eventually outgrow the condition.

116

30. Retinal disparity
    a. is an abnormal condition that should be treated as early as possible.
    b. is a cue for depth perception only in people with strabismus.
    c. can be used as a cue for depth perception no matter what the organism's early experience was.
    d. can be used for stereoscopic depth perception because cortical cells respond differentially to the degree of retinal disparity.

31. Nerve growth factor (NGF), if injected in large amounts into the brains of infant rats with strabismus,
    a. allowed for normal development of stereoscopic depth perception.
    b. destroyed the ability to detect movement.
    c. made the animals blind.
    d. resulted in inability to use the fovea.

32. While recording from cortical cells in kittens whose eyes were opened immediately before recording, Hubel and Wiesel found that:
    a. there were simple cortical cells, but no complex cells.
    b. there were complex cortical cells, but no simple cells.
    c. simple and complex cells had receptive field properties similar to those of adult cats.
    d. the cells were more active than in adult cats.

33. Experiments on abnormal sensory environments have shown that:
    a. if kittens are reared in an environment in which they see only horizontal lines, at maturity all cells are completely normal, because receptive field characteristics are fully determined at birth.
    b. if kittens are reared with only horizontal lines, they will lose the ability to see vertical lines.
    c. if kittens are reared with only horizontal lines, they will become so habituated to that stimulus that they soon lose their ability to see horizontal lines.
    d. if the environment is illuminated only with a strobe light during development, kittens lose their ability to see colors.

34. Astigmatism
    a. is caused by too much retinal disparity and results in loss of depth perception.
    b. is caused by strabismus and results in color blindness.
    c. is caused by amblyopia and results in loss of binocular cells in the cortex.
    d. is caused by asymmetric curvature of the eyes and results in blurring of vision for lines in one direction.

Answers to Multiple-Choice Questions

1. c	10. c	19. c	28. a
2. a	11. b	20. d	29. b
3. c	12. b	21. d	30. d
4. b	13. a	22. a	31. a
5. b	14. c	23. b	32. c
6. a	15. d	24. c	33. b
7. d	16. a	25. a	34. d
8. a	17. d	26. d	
9. d	18. b	27. c	

Diagrams

1. In the diagram of the retina below, label the following parts of the receptors: cell body, synaptic pedicle, inner segment, outer segment. Then label the receptors with an "R" in the cell body. Similarly, label the horizontal cell with an "H," bipolar cells with "B," amacrine cells with "A," ganglion cells with "G." Label the optic nerve fibers.

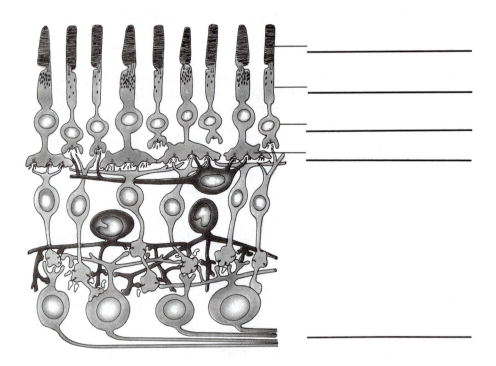

2. Label the following components of the vision pathways on this horizontal section of the brain: optic nerve, optic chiasm, lateral geniculate nucleus, primary visual cortex, superior colliculus.

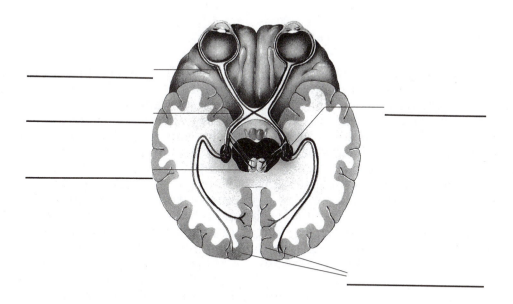

3. Does the following diagram represent the response characteristics of a retinal ganglion cell, a lateral geniculate cell, a "simple" cortical cell, or a "complex" cortical cell?

High response

Low response

High response

Low response

High response

7

THE NONVISUAL SENSORY SYSTEMS

INTRODUCTION

Sensory systems have evolved to provide information most useful for each species. Although humans can perceive a relatively wide range of stimuli, our sensory systems also show certain specializations.

The sense of hearing uses air vibrations to move the tympanic membrane and three middle ear bones (the hammer, anvil, and stirrup), which focus the force of the vibrations so that they can move the heavier fluid inside the cochlea. The basilar membrane forms the floor of a tunnel, the scala media. Receptor cells are embedded in the basilar membrane; hairs in the top of the receptors are in contact with the overlying tectorial membrane. Inward pressure of the stirrup on the oval window increases pressure in scala vestibuli, which presses down on scala media, which in turn bulges downward into scala tympani and pushes the round window outward. The opposite happens when the stirrup moves outward. The movement of the basilar membrane (the floor of scala media) relative to the tectorial membrane bends the hair cells, thereby generating a potential. The characteristics of the basilar membrane vary along the length of the cochlea. At the basal end a bony shelf occupies most of the floor of scala media, and the basilar membrane, which attaches to the shelf, is thin and stiff. At the apex, there is almost no bony shelf, and the basilar membrane is larger and floppier, even though the cochlea as a whole is smaller. The size and stiffness of the basilar membrane determine which part of the basilar membrane will respond to various frequencies of sound with the greatest-amplitude traveling wave. High-pitched tones cause maximal displacement near the base, and low-pitched tones cause maximal displacement closer to the apex.

Pitch perception depends on a combination of three mechanisms. At low frequencies, neurons can fire with each vibration. At medium frequencies, neurons split into volleys, one volley firing with one vibration, another with the next, and so on. At higher frequencies the area of the basilar membrane with greatest displacement is used as a place code. There is considerable overlap of pitches coded by frequency of firing and by place.

There are two categories of hearing impairment. Nerve, or inner ear, deafness is caused by damage to the cochlea, the hair cells, or the auditory nerve. Prenatal infections or toxins, inadequate oxygen during birth, childhood diseases or reactions to drugs, and exposure to loud noises are frequent causes of nerve deafness. Conductive, or middle ear, deafness results from failure of the middle ear bones to transmit sound waves to the cochlea. It can be causes by diseases, infections, or tumorous growths in the middle ear.

Sound localization is accomplished by two methods. The difference in loudness between the two ears is used for high-frequency (short-wavelength) sounds, while the phase difference for sound waves arriving at the two ears is used for low-frequency (long-wavelength) sounds. However, for animals with small heads, there is little phase difference in the sound waves reaching the two ears. Therefore, it is difficult for them to localize low frequency tones. Furthermore, they can use loudness differences only for higher frequencies than humans can. These animals have evolved the ability to perceive sounds that they can localize easily. The lateral part of the superior olive, in the medulla, mediates localization based on loudness differences, whereas the medial part subserves localization based on phase differences.

Vestibular sensation, based on the otolith organs and the semicircular canals in the inner ear, contributes to our sense of balance. Our auditory system, and perhaps other mechanical systems, including the vestibular system, may have evolved from the lateral line system of primitive fish.

The sense of touch is composed of several modalities, some of which are fairly well correlated with activity in specific receptor types. For example, free nerve endings are involved in sensations of pain, warmth, and cold. Hair follicle receptors respond to movement of hairs; Meissner's corpuscles and Pacinian corpuscles signal sudden displacement of skin. Merkel's disks produce a prolonged response to steady indentation of the skin, while Ruffini endings respond to skin stretching. Although itching sensations are carried by the same spinal nerves that carry pain information, the receptors that generate itching are not known, and the painkiller morphine does not inhibit itching.

Sensory nerves enter and motor nerves exit the spinal cord through each of 31 openings in the vertebral canal. These nerves innervate overlapping segments of the body (dermatomes). Several well defined pathways ascend from the spinal cord to separate areas of the thalamus, and thence to appropriate areas of somatosensory cortex. Thus, the various aspects of somatosensation are at least partially separated from the receptor level to the cerebral cortex. Since bodily sensations depend on activity in the cerebral cortex, some people may experience a "phantom limb" after a part of the body has been amputated. In other patients damage to the somatosensory cortex may result in loss of sensation in certain parts of their bodies.

According to the gate theory, various kinds of nonpain stimuli can modify pain sensations. Pain information is transmitted to the spinal cord by axons with little or no myelin, using substance P as their transmitter. From the spinal cord, pain information is sent to the ventrobasal nucleus of the thalamus, and then to the cingulate cortex and somatosensory cortex. Capsaicin, derived from hot peppers, elicits the release of substance P and thereby produces a sensation of pain or heat. However, following application of capsaicin, there is a prolonged decrease in pain sensations. Pain sensations can be counteracted by release of the brain's endogenous opiates (endorphins), including leu- and met-enkephalin, beta-endorphin, and dynorphin. The enkephalins are released locally as neurotransmitters; beta-endorphin and dynorphin are released as hormones from the pituitary into the blood-stream, but they may also serve as neurotransmitters. Enkephalins are concentrated in the periaqueductal gray area of the brain stem, where they may block the release of substance P. Several stimuli can elicit the release of endorphins; these include pain, stress, acupuncture, and transcutaneous electrical nerve stimulation. However, some types of analgesia are dependent, not on endorphins, but on activity at certain glutamate synapses. Morphine administered for serious pain is almost never addictive. Furthermore, although opiates inhibit the immune system temporarily, prolonged pain or stress weakens the immune system for a much longer time.

Our understanding of the senses of taste and olfaction is plagued with many unresolved issues. There is lack of agreement as to whether there are a fixed number of primary stimuli, which send information to the brain via "labeled lines," or whether the brain analyzes patterns of firing across whole populations of neurons, with sensations varying along continuous dimensions. Compromises between the two positions will probably be required for both senses, but the exact nature of the compromises has not been specified. Studies of cross adaptation suggest that we have at least four types of taste receptor: sweet, sour, salty, and bitter. There may also be a receptor for monosodium glutamate and additional receptors for bitter and sweet. The mechanisms of activation of some taste receptors have been discovered. Sodium ions activate salty receptors; acids close potassium channels in sour receptors; and sweetness and bitterness receptors respond to molecules that activate G proteins, which then release a second messenger within the cell. The anterior two-thirds of the tongue sends information via the chorda tympani, a branch of the seventh cranial nerve (facial nerve) to the nucleus solitarius in the medulla. The posterior third of the tongue and the throat send input via branches of the ninth and tenth cranial nerves to different parts of the nucleus solitarius. From there the information is sent to numerous areas, including the pons, lateral hypothalamus, amygdala, ventral-posterior thalamus, and two areas of the cerebral cortex. The nucleus solitarius in rats, and the cerebral cortex in monkeys, can respond differentially according to the acceptability of a taste.

Olfactory cells have cilia that extend into the mucous lining of the nasal passages. Odorant molecules must diffuse through a mucous fluid in order to reach the receptor sites, which are probably on the cilia. There may be 100 or more olfactory receptor proteins, which operate on the same principles as some neurotransmitter receptors. When activated by an odorant molecule, the receptor triggers a change in a G protein, which in turn elicits chemical activities within the cell. People with specific anosmias lack one or more of these receptors. Because there are so many types of receptor, olfaction has more of a labeled-line system of coding than does, for example, color vision, which has only three types of cones. However, even in olfaction, each receptor responds to other odorants that are similar to its preferred stimulus. Therefore, a single receptor can provide an approximate classification of an odorant, but related receptors provide more exact information.

KEY TERMS AND CONCEPTS

Audition
1. Sound
    Amplitude
        Loudness
    Frequency
        Pitch

2. Structures of the ear
    Tympanic membrane
    Middle ear bones
        Hammer (malleus)
        Anvil (incus)
        Stirrup (stapes)
    Oval window
    Cochlea
        Scala vestibuli
        Scala tympani
        Scala media
            Basilar membrane
            Hair cells
            Tectorial membrane

3. Pitch perception
    Frequency theory
        Volley principle
    Place theory
        Base: thin, stiff basilar membrane
        Apex: larger, floppier basilar membrane
        Traveling wave

4. Deafness
    Nerve deafness
        Inner-ear deafness

Conductive deafness
    Middle-ear deafness

5.   Localization of sounds
    Difference in loudness
        Sound shadow
        High pitches
        Lateral part of superior olive
    Difference in time of arrival
        Phase difference
        Low pitches
        Medial part of superior olive

The mechanical senses
1.   Lateral line system

2.   Vestibular sensation
    Otolith organs
    Semicircular canals
    Eighth cranial nerve
    Brain stem and cerebellum

3.   Somatosensation
    Receptors
        Free nerve endings
        Hair-follicle receptors
        Meissner's corpuscles
        Pacinian corpuscles
        Merkel's disks
        Ruffini endings
        Krause end bulbs
    Spinal cord and brain
        31 sets of spinal nerves
        Dermatome
        Somatosensory thalamus
        Somatosensory cortex
            Parietal lobe
            Four parallel strips
            Phantom limbs
            Impaired sense of body parts

4.   Pain
    Gate theory
    Pain neurons and neurotransmitters
        Substance P
        Capsaicin

Opiates and endorphins
    Enkephalins
    Beta-endorphin
    Dynorphin
    Periaqueductal gray area
Stimuli that produce analgesia
    Pain or stress
        Naloxone
        Glutamate (nonendorphin) analgesia
    Acupuncture
    Transcutaneous nerve stimulation
Pros and cons of morphine analgesia
    Rarely addicitve
    Less inhibition of immune system than pain

The chemical senses
1.   Chemical coding
    Labeled lines
    Across-fiber pattern

2.   Taste
    Taste receptors
        Taste buds
        Papillae
    Kinds of taste receptors
        Cross adaptation
        Four main types: sweet, sour, salty, bitter
        Other possibilities
            Monosodium glutamate
            Multiple bitter and sweet receptors
    Mechanisms of taste receptors
        Salty: sodium influx
            Amiloride
            Bretylium tosylate
        Sour: acid closes potassium channels
        Sweet: G protein and second messenger
        Bitter: G protein and second messenger
    Coding of taste
        Labeled-line theory
        Across-fiber pattern theory
    Taste coding in the brain
        Seventh cranial nerve (facial)
        Nucleus solitarius
        Acceptability of a taste

3. Olfaction
    Olfactory receptors
        Olfactory cells
            Replaceable
        Olfactory epithelium
        Cilia
        Mucous fluid
        Olfactory bulb
        Cerebral cortex, hippocampus, amygdala, hypothalamus
    Behavioral methods to identify olfactory receptors
        Specific anosmias
    Biochemical identification of receptor types
        Similar to neurotransmitter receptors
            Seven transmembrane sections
            G proteins
        Possibly 100 or more receptor proteins
    Implications for coding
        "Preferred" odor
        Mostly labeled-line
        Some across-fiber pattern
    Pheromone

SHORT-ANSWER QUESTIONS

Audition
1. *Sound*
    a. What is the relationship between amplitude and loudness? between frequency and pitch?

2. *Structures of the ear*
    a. What is the role of the tympanic membrane and the hammer, anvil, and stirrup?

b. Where are the auditory receptors located? How are they stimulated?

3. *Pitch perception*
    a. What led to the downfall of the frequency theory of pitch discrimination in its simple form?

    b. What is the volley theory?

    c. What observations led to the downfall of the place theory as Helmholtz stated it?

    d. What is the current compromise between the place and frequency theories of pitch discrimination?

e.   At which end of the cochlea is the basilar membrane stiffest?

f.   How does the traveling wave along the basilar membrane lead to place coding?

4. *Deafness*
   a.   For what type of deafness is hearing impaired for a limited range of frequencies?

   b.   For which type of deafness can one hear one's own voice, though external sounds are heard poorly?

   c.   What are some causes of nerve deafness? of conductive deafness?

5. *Sound localization*
   a. For which frequencies is the "sound shadow" method of localization best? Why?

   b. What is the other major method of sound localization? For which frequencies is it most effective?

   c. Which method of sound localization is best for a species with a small head? Why?

   d. Where is the superior olive? Would the lateral or the medial part be better developed in a small-headed species?

The mechanical senses
1. *The lateral line system*
   a. Describe the lateral line system of fish. To what type of stimuli do its receptors respond? Which of our senses probably evolved from the lateral line system?

2. *Vestibular sensation*
   a. What are the main parts of the vestibular organ? What are otoliths? What is their function?

   b. What are the semicircular canals? How do they differ from the otolith organs?

3. *Somatosensation*
   a. List the somatosensory receptors and their probable functions.

   b. How many sets of spinal nerves do we have?

   c. What is a dermatome?

d.   Describe briefly the cortical projections of the somatosensory system.

e.   Why do some people feel phantom limbs after loss of a limb?

f.   Describe the loss of body sense that may accompany Alzheimer's disease.

4.   *Pain*
   a.   What theory did Melzack and Wall propose to account for the variations in pain responsiveness? What is its main principle?

   b.   What is substance P? What sensation would be produced by an injection of substance P into the spinal cord?

c. What is capsaicin? How does it work? What food contains capsaicin?

d. What are endorphins? How was the term derived?

e. What are enkephalins? Which two endorphins may serve as either hormones or neurotransmitters?

f. Where are enkephalin synapses concentrated? What is their probable mode of action there?

g. List four kinds of stimuli that can reduce pain.

h. What is naloxone? How is it used experimentally?

i. What neurotransmitter may mediate nonendorphin analgesia?

j. What are the pros and cons of morphine analgesia in cases of serious pain?

The chemical senses
1. *General issues about chemical coding*
    a. Describe the labeled line type of coding. Give an example.

    b. Describe the across-fiber pattern type of coding. Give an example.

2. *Taste*
   a. Where are the taste receptors located? What is the relationship between taste buds and papillae?

   b. How can cross adaptation be used to help determine the number of taste receptors?

   c. What are the four major kinds of taste receptor? What additional kinds may we have?

   d. What are the mechanisms of activation of salty, sour, sweet, and bitter receptors? How do amiloride and bretylium affect salty tastes?

   e. What evidence favors the labeled-line theory of taste? the across-fiber pattern theory?

f.   Which structures in the brain process taste information?

g.   What property, other than the physical identity of tastes, is classified by the nucleus solitarius of rats? Which area performs this function in monkeys?

3.   *Olfaction*
a.   Describe the olfactory receptors. Why is there a delay between inhaling a substance and smelling it?

b.   What is a specific anosmia? What can we conclude about the number of olfactory receptors, based on information about specific anosmias?

c.   How are olfactory receptors similar to neurotransmitter receptors? How many olfactory receptor proteins are estimated to exist, based on isolation of these proteins?

d.   What can we say about the labeled-line theory vs. the across-fiber pattern theory for smell?

POSTTEST

Multiple-Choice Questions

1. Which of the following is true of auditory perception?
    a.   Loudness is the same thing as amplitude.
    b.   Pitch is the perception of intensity.
    c.   Perception of high frequencies improves with age.
    d.   The upper limit for hearing decreases in middle-aged adults by about 80 Hz every six months.

2. The function of the tympanic membrane and middle-ear bones is to
    a.   directly stimulate the auditory receptors.
    b.   move the tectorial membrane to which the stirrup is connected.
    c.   focus the vibrations on a small area, so that there is sufficient force to produce pressure waves in the fluid-filled cochlea.
    d.   none of the above.

3. The auditory receptors
    a.   are called hair cells.
    b.   are embedded in the basilar membrane below and the tectorial membrane above.
    c.   are stimulated when the scala media is pushed up and down by pressure waves, thereby bending the hair cells between the basilar membrane and the tectorial membrane.
    d.   all of the above.

4. The frequency theory
    a.   cannot describe coding of high-frequency tones because the refractory periods of neurons limit their firing rates.
    b.   can be modified by the volley principle to account for pitch discrimination of all frequencies.
    c.   is now thought to be valid for high-frequency tones, whereas the place theory describes pitch coding of lower tones.
    d.   is a form of labeled-line theory.

5. The place theory
    a. received experimental support from Helmholtz, who demonstrated that the basilar membrane did indeed operate like a series of piano strings.
    b. has been modified so that a traveling wave produces a greater displacement at one area of the basilar membrane than at others.
    c. cannot be true at all, because the basilar membrane is the same throughout its entire length and therefore cannot localize vibrations.
    d. cannot be true at all, because the basilar membrane is too loose and floppy to show any localization.

6. The basilar membrane
    a. is smallest and stiffest at its apex at the farthest (small) end of the cochlea.
    b. is smallest and stiffest at its base at the large end of the cochlea.
    c. has the same dimensions and consistency throughout its length.
    d. shows maximum displacement for low tones near its base.

7. Pitch discrimination
    a. depends on a combination of mechanisms: frequency coding for low pitches, a modified version of place coding for high pitches, and both mechanisms for intermediate pitches.
    b. depends on a combination of mechanisms: frequency coding for high pitches, a modified version of place coding for low pitches, and both mechanisms for intermediate pitches.
    c. cannot be satisfactorily explained by any theory.
    d. is accomplished only by place coding.

8. Inner-ear deafness
    a. is frequently temporary; if it persists it can usually be corrected by surgery.
    b. is characterized by total deafness to all sounds.
    c. may result from exposure of one's mother to rubella or other contagious diseases during pregnancy.
    d. is characterized by being able to hear one's own voice but not external sounds.

9. A "sound shadow"
    a. is useful for sound localization only for low-pitched sounds.
    b. is useful for sound localization only for wavelengths shorter than the width of the head (that is, higher pitches).
    c. is used by the auditory cortex to localize sounds.
    d. cannot be used at all by small-headed species.

10. The superior olive
    a. is located in the cochlea.
    b. contributes to sound localization only by loudness differences.
    c. lacks a structure equivalent to the medial superior olive in small-headed species such as mice, because these species cannot use phase differences to localize stimuli.
    d. is used for pitch discrimination but not localization of sounds.

11. The lateral line organ of fish
    a. is a row of receptors on each side of the body that detect the fish's own movement.
    b. is probably the evolutionary precursor to our olfactory cells.
    c. is a row of receptors in the inner ear of fish that detect sounds in the water.
    d. is a row of touch receptors on each side of the body that detect vibrations in the water.

12. Vestibular sensation
    a. arises from free nerve endings in the inner ear.
    b. is produced by a traveling wave along a membrane in the otolith organs.
    c. arises from hair cells in the otolith organs and the semicircular canals.
    d. plays only a minor role in balance and coordination.

13. Which of the following pairs of receptors and sensations is most correct?
    a. free nerve endings: pain, warmth, cold
    b. Merkel's disks: sudden movement across skin
    c. Pacinian corpuscles: steady indentation of skin
    d. Ruffini endings: itching

14. Dermatomes
    a. are sharply defined, nonoverlapping areas innervated by single sensory spinal nerves.
    b. are overlapping areas innervated by single sensory spinal nerves.
    c. are symptoms of a skin disorder, much like acne.
    d. are found only on the trunk of the body, not the arms, legs, or head.

15. Somatosensory information
    a. travels up a single pathway to one thalamic nucleus, which projects to one strip in the parietal lobe.
    b. travels up different pathways to end in at least four thalamic areas, which project to four parallel strips in the parietal lobe.
    c. travels directly from the spinal cord to the parietal lobe, without any synapses on the way.
    d. travels to four thalamic areas, which project to four parallel strips in the temporal lobe.

16. Phantom limbs
    a. result from activity in the cerebral cortex that used to be associated with the lost body part.
    b. are rarely experienced for more than a day or two after loss of the body part.
    c. result from the subconscious desire to regain the body part.
    d. are a frequent symptom of Alzheimer's disease.

17. The gate theory of pain
    a. was proposed by Melzack and Wall.
    b. states that nonpain input can close the "gates" for pain messages.
    c. may explain why athletes and soldiers may report little pain from a serious injury.
    d. all of the above.

18. Substance P
    a. is released in the spinal cord by unmyelinated and thinly myelinated axons carrying pain information.
    b. activates receptors that can be blocked by capsaicin.
    c. is an endogenous opiate.
    d. none of the above.

19. Leu- and met-enkephalin
    a. have chemical structures virtually identical to morphine.
    b. are released from the pituitary into the blood.
    c. are peptide neurotransmitters, consisting of five amino acids each, that have opiate-like effects.
    d. all of the above.

20. Which of the following is true of the periaqueductal gray area?
    a. It contains numerous enkephalin synapses.
    b. Stimulation of enkephalin receptors there blocks release of substance P in pain pathways.
    c. Electrical stimulation there produces analgesia.
    d. All of the above are true.

21. Naloxone
    a. is one of the enkephalins.
    b. blocks opiate receptors.
    c. is released by transcutaneous nerve stimulation.
    d. depletes substance P.

22. Which of the following is true of analgesia?
    a. All forms are blocked by naloxone.
    b. Morphine administered for serious pain is especially addictive, and should be avoided.
    c. Certain glutamate synapses inhibit some kinds of pain.
    d. Morphine seriously weakens the immune system for as long as it is administered.

23. The labeled-line theory
    a. states that each receptor responds to a wide range of stimuli and contributes to the perception of every stimulus in its system.
    b. describes pitch coding for high frequency tones.
    c. describes color coding.
    d. all of the above.

24. Which of the following is true concerning taste receptors and neurons?
    a. Each receptor has its own taste bud and its own neuronal fiber.
    b. There are about two to three receptors in each taste bud, and each receptor has its own neuronal fiber.
    c. There are about 50 receptors in each taste bud, and each neuron receives synaptic contacts from a number of receptors.
    d. There is only one receptor per taste bud, but each receptor on the tongue makes contact with numerous neurons.

25. Cross adaptation studies have suggested that
    a. there are at least four kinds of taste receptors.
    b. there may be a separate receptor for monosodium glutamate.
    c. there may be more than one kind of receptor for both bitter and sweet tastes.
    d. all of the above.

26. Which of the following is an appropriate pairing of receptor type with its method of activation?
    a. salty: sodium inflow
    b. sweet: closing potassium channels
    c. sour: activation of G protein
    d. bitter: sodium outflow

27. Bretylium tosylate
    a. facilitates sodium flow across the membrane and intensifies salty tastes.
    b. blocks sodium flow across the membrane and intensifies salty tastes.
    c. blocks sodium flow across the membrane and reduces the intensity of salty tastes
    d. facilitates potassium flow across the membrane and intensifies sweet tastes

28. The across-fiber pattern theory of taste
    a. assumes that there are seven basic taste qualities.
    b. holds that taste is coded in terms of a pattern of neural activity across a great many neurons.
    c. has been disproven by the finding that every receptor responds only to one taste.
    d. none of the above.

29. The nucleus solitarius
    a. is located in the cerebral cortex and projects to the medulla.
    b. is located in the medulla and projects to the pons, lateral hypothalamus, amygdala, thalamus, and cerebral cortex.
    c. is located in the medulla and sends its output primarily to cranial nerves.
    d. is responsible only for information about the physical identity of substances; acceptability of tastes is classified only at the level of the cerebral cortex, even in rats.

30. Olfactory receptors
    a. are not replaceable, once they die.
    b. each respond to only one specific odor.
    c. respond equally well to a great many odors.
    d. have cilia that extend into the mucous surface of the nasal passage; odorant molecules must pass through the mucus to reach the receptor site.

31. Specific anosmias
    a. are usually very debilitating.
    b. have shown that there are only 4 kinds of olfactory receptors.
    c. suggest that there are probably a fairly large number of kinds of olfactory receptors.
    d. suggest that there are no "preferred" stimuli for olfactory receptors; identification of odors depends entirely on an across-fiber pattern code.

32. Isolation of olfactory receptor molecules has shown that
   a. olfactory receptors are similar to neurotransmitter receptors in that they have seven transmembrane sections.
   b. olfactory receptors are similar to neurotransmitter receptors in that they trigger changes in a G protein, which then provokes chemical activities inside the cell.
   c. there are at least 18, and probably 100 or more, olfactory receptor proteins.
   d. all of the above.

Answers to Multiple-Choice Questions

1. d	7. a	13. a	19. c	25. d	31. c
2. c	8. c	14. b	20. d	26. a	32. d
3. d	9. b	15. b	21. b	27. a	
4. a	10. c	16. a	22. c	28. b	
5. b	11. d	17. d	23. b	29. b	
6. b	12. c	18. a	24. c	30. d	

Diagrams

1. Label the following structures of the ear: external auditory canal, tympanic membrane (ear drum), hammer, anvil, stirrup, cochlea, auditory nerve.

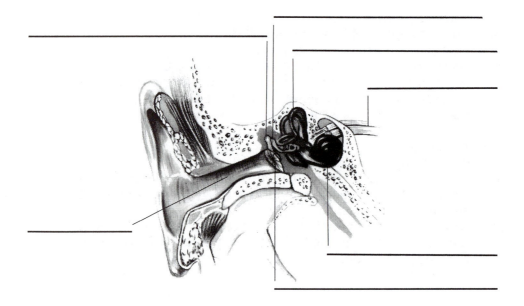

2. Label the following structures of the inner ear: basilar membrane, hair cell, cochlear neuron.

_____   _____

3. Label the following structures: olfactory bulb, olfactory epithelium, olfactory receptor cells, supporting cells, olfactory cilia (dendrites), olfactory nerve axons.

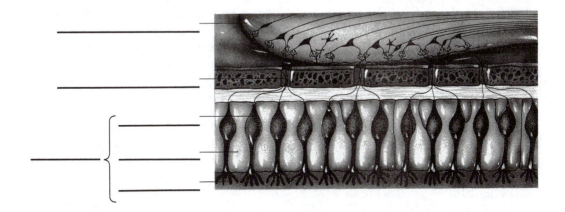

8

MOVEMENT

INTRODUCTION

All movements of the body result from muscle contractions. Acetylcholine is the neurotransmitter released at the neuromuscular junction; it always results in contraction of the recipient muscle. We manage to move our limbs in two opposite directions by alternately contracting antagonistic muscles, such as flexors and extensors. There are three categories of muscle: smooth, skeletal (or striated), and cardiac. Skeletal muscles are in turn divided into three types: red, slow, fatigue-resistant; pink, intermediate-speed, moderately fatigue-resistant; and white, fast, easily fatigued. Muscles consist of many fibers, each of which is innervated by one axon; however, each axon can innervate more than one fiber. Greater precision of movement can be achieved if each axon innervates few muscle fibers.

Two kinds of receptors signal change in the state of muscle contraction. The muscle spindle is a stretch receptor located in fibers parallel to the main muscle. Whenever the main muscle and spindle are stretched, the spindle sends impulses to the spinal cord that excite the motor neurons innervating the main muscle. This results in contraction of the main muscle, opposing the original stretch. The Golgi tendon organ is located at both ends of the main muscle and responds to increased tension in the muscle, as when the muscle is contracting or being actively stretched by an external stimulus. Its impulses to the spinal cord inhibit the motor neuron, leading to relaxation of the muscle. Combinations of activity in these two receptors allow one to maintain steady positions, to resist external forces, and to monitor voluntary movement.

Most behaviors are complex mixtures of voluntary and involuntary, or reflexive, components. Some movements are ballistic, which means that they proceed automatically once triggered. Oscillators are repetitive alternations of more-or-less ballistic movements, such as wing flapping in birds or scratching in dogs. Other movements require constant sensory feedback. Motor programs are large coordinated chunks of movements; they may be learned or innate. Fixed action patterns are species-specific motor programs that develop almost automatically.

The spinal cord receives sensory nerves entering dorsally and projects motor axons from its ventral side. In addition, it contains motor programs that direct the specific muscle movements for common behaviors such as walking, running, and scratching. The cerebellum is important for learning, planning and coordinating complex movements, especially rapid sequences that require accurate timing and aiming. Parallel fibers in the cerebellar cortex activate Purkinje cells, which in turn inhibit the cerebellar nuclei. Since a major function of these nuclei is to hold parts of the body steady, inhibiting them for shorter or longer times determines the duration and distance of a ballistic movement. Damage to the cerebellum impairs rapid alternating movements, saccades, and the ability to touch one's nose with one's finger.

The basal ganglia are a group of subcortical structures that control the direction and distance of movements, especially postural movements. They also contribute to the planning of such movements. They consist of the caudate nucleus, putamen, globus pallidus, substantia nigra, and subthalamic nucleus.

The cerebral cortex coordinates complex plans of movement. The primary motor cortex contributes the greatest output to the spinal cord; each area controls a different part of the body. It is in turn guided by input from prefrontal, premotor, and supplementary motor cortex, all of which are active during the planning of a movement. There are several ways of dividing the cortical systems that control movement. One such division is between the pyramidal and extrapyramidal systems. The pyramidal system originates in primary motor cortex and adjacent areas and descends to the medulla, where its axons cross to the opposite side in swellings called the pyramids, from which the system gets its name. These axons extend without synapsing to motor neurons or interneurons in the medulla and spinal cord; they are also referred to as the corticospinal tract.

The extrapyramidal system consists of all the motor areas that are not part of the pyramidal system; these include widespread areas of the cerebral cortex, the basal ganglia, the red nucleus, the reticular formation, and the vestibular nucleus. The side effects of certain drugs include clumsiness and poor motor coordination; these are called extrapyramidal symptoms, because they resemble the effects of damage to the basal ganglia and other extrapyramidal structures.

Another division of motor systems is that between the dorsolateral and the ventrolateral tracts. The dorsolateral tract includes fibers of the pyramidal system and the red nucleus, all of which cross from one side to the other. It controls movements in the periphery of the opposite side of the body. The ventromedial tract consists of the remaining fibers from the cortex as well as those from the reticular formation and vestibular nucleus, none of which cross within the brain. However, when they reach the spinal cord, they contact cells that branch to both sides of the cord. They control movements near the midline of the body that require bilateral control.

Myasthenia gravis is a disease characterized by weakness and fatigue. It results from autoimmune destruction of acetylcholine receptors on muscle fibers. It may be treated either with immune-suppressant drugs or with drugs that inhibit the enzyme acetylcholinesterase, which breaks down acetylcholine. The symptoms of Parkinson's disease include slow movement, difficulty initiating movements, muscle rigidity and tremor, and sometimes intellectual impairment and depression. Parkinson's disease results from degeneration of dopamine neurons ascending from the substantia nigra in the midbrain to the caudate nucleus and putamen, which are part of the basal ganglia. Its symptoms can be lessened with L-DOPA, the precursor of dopamine, although such treatment frequently results in undesirable side effects. One possible cause of this disease is MPTP in the environment, possibly in the form of paraquat, an herbicide. In order for MPTP to destroy the dopaminergic neurons, it must first be converted to MPP^+ by the enzyme monoamine oxidase B. This enzyme can be inhibited by deprenyl; treatment with deprenyl has been shown to slow the progress of Parkinson's disease.

Whereas Parkinson's disease results from degeneration of the dopaminergic input to the basal ganglia, Huntington's disease results from degeneration of the postsynaptic neurons there. However, since many types of cells are lost, no single therapy is very successful. Symptoms begin with a facial twitch and progressively lead to tremors in other parts of the body and finally to total inability to move. The immediate cause of the degeneration may be overstimulation of excitatory glutamate receptors by chemicals similar to kainic acid or quinolinic acid. A dominant autosomal gene on chromosome 4 has been identified as the ultimate cause of the disease. In people with Huntington's disease this gene contains extra repetitions of a sequence of bases in the genetic code for a protein; however, no one knows what this protein does or how the extra repetitions alter its function.

KEY TERMS AND CONCEPTS

The control of movement
1. Muscles and their movements
   Categories of muscle
      Smooth
      Skeletal or striated
      Cardiac
   Neuromuscular junction
      Acetylcholine
      Muscle contraction
   Antagonistic muscles
      Flexor
      Extensor
   Relation of sensory and motor nerves to spinal cord
      Sensory nerves enter dorsally
      Motor nerves exit ventrally
   Fast and slow skeletal muscles
      Slow, red, resistant to fatigue
      Intermediate speed, pink, moderately resistant to fatigue
      Fast, forceful, white, fatigue quickly

Muscle control by proprioceptors
>Stretch reflex
>Muscle spindle
>Golgi tendon organ

2. Units of movement
Voluntary and involuntary movements
>Reflexes
Movements with high or low sensitivity to feedback
>Ballistic movement
>Oscillators
>>Scratch reflex
>High sensitivity to feedback
>>Threading needle
>>Singing
>>>Delayed auditory feedback
Skilled and unskilled movements
>Motor program
>Fixed action pattern

Brain mechanisms of movement

1. The role of the spinal cord
Motor programs for walking and scratching
Rhythm generator

2. The role of the cerebellum
Learned motor responses
Effects of damage to the cerebellum
>Inability to link motions rapidly and smoothly
Tests of cerebellar functioning
>Saccades
>Finger-to-nose test
>>Move function: cerebellar cortex
>>Hold function: cerebellar nuclei
Cellular organization of the cerebellum
>Cerebellar cortex
>>Parallel fibers activate Purkinje cells
>>Purkinje cells inhibit cerebellar nuclei
>Cerebellar nuclei
>Thalamus to motor areas of cerebral cortex
>Red nucleus in midbrain

3. The role of the basal ganglia
Component structures
>Caudate nucleus
>Putamen

Globus pallidus
Substantia nigra
Subthalamic nucleus
Output to primary motor cortex
Functions
Direction and distance of movement
Postural adjustments
Planning and organizing movements

4. The role of the cerebral cortex
Overall plans of movement
Fritsch and Hitzig
Electrical stimulation
The primary motor cortex and neighboring areas
Primary motor cortex
Somatosensory cortex
Prefrontal cortex
Premotor cortex
Supplementary motor cortex
The coding of movement in the primary motor cortex
Map of parts of body
Direction of movement
Movement vector
Connections from the brain to the spinal cord
The pyramidal system (corticospinal tract)
Primary motor cortex and adjacent areas
Pyramids in medulla
The extrapyramidal system
Diffuse areas of cortex
Basal ganglia
Red nucleus
Reticular formation
Vestibular nucleus
Extrapyramidal symptoms
Dorsolateral tract of spinal cord
Axons of pyramidal system and red nucleus
Controls peripheral movements on opposite side of body
Ventromedial tract of spinal cord
Uncrossed axons from cortex, reticular formation and
vestibular nucleus
Contacts bilaterally branched spinal neurons
Controls midline movements requiring bilateral influence

Disorders of movement
1. Myasthenia gravis
Autoimmune destruction of acetylcholine receptors

Progressive weakness and fatigue
Treatments
    Suppress immune system
    Inhibit acetylcholinesterase

2. Parkinson's disease
    Extrapyramidal disorder
    Symptoms
        Slow movements
        Difficulty initiating movements
        Rigidity of muscles
        Tremors
        Sometimes intellectual impairment and depressed mood
    Degeneration of dopamine axons from substantia nigra to caudate
        nucleus and putamen
    Possible causes of Parkinson's disease
        Some weak genetic predisposition
        Interruption of blood flow to some brain areas
        Encephalitis or other viral infections
        Prolonged exposure to certain drugs or toxic substances
            MPTP, MPPP, MPP$^+$
            Herbicides, pesticides (including paraquat)
    L-DOPA treatment
        Precursor to dopamine
        Side effects
    New therapies
        Monoamine oxidase B inhibitors
            Deprenyl

3. Huntington's disease (Huntington's chorea)
    Symptoms
        Twitches and tremors
        Slow and clumsy voluntary movements
        Psychological symptoms
    Nature of brain damage
        Loss of neurons in basal ganglia and cortex
        Kainic acid or quinolinic acid
            Stimulate glutamate receptors
            Damage neurons by overstimulation
    Heredity and presymptomatic testing
        Autosomal dominant gene
        Chromosome #4
        Extra repetitions of sequence of bases

SHORT-ANSWER QUESTIONS

The control of movement

1. *Muscles and their movements*

   a.   List the three categories of muscle.

   b.   What is the transmitter at the neuromuscular junction? What is its effect? How do we move our limbs in two opposite directions?

   c.   What is the relationship of sensory and motor nerves to the spinal cord? Where are the cell bodies and axon terminals of the motor neurons?

   d.   List the types and functions of skeletal muscle.

   e.   Contrast the muscles of sprinters and marathon runners.

f. What is a proprioceptor? a stretch reflex? Does the stretch reflex cause or result from a stretch of the muscle?

g. What is a muscle spindle? What is its effect on the spinal motor neuron that innervates its associated muscle?

h. Explain the knee-jerk reflex in terms of the above mechanism.

i. What is a Golgi tendon organ? What is its effect on the spinal motor neuron that innervates its associated muscle? What is its functional role?

2. *Units of movement*
    a. What is a reflex?

b.   Describe some of the involuntary components of "voluntary" behaviors, such as walking or talking.

c.   What is a ballistic movement?

d.   What is an oscillator? Give two examples.

e.   What is the effect of delayed auditory feedback on a singer's ability to hold a single note for a long time?

f.   What is a motor program? Give examples of "built-in" and learned motor programs.

g.   What is a fixed action pattern? Give an example. Do humans
     have any built-in motor patterns?

Brain mechanisms of movement
1.   *The role of the spinal cord*
     a.   Where is the rhythm generator for the cat's scratch reflex?
          What happens to the rhythm generator if the muscles are
          paralyzed?

2.   *The role of the cerebellum*
     a.   Describe the role of the cerebellum in movement. What is the
          evidence that it helps to plan, as well as execute, movements?

     b.   What kinds of movements are especiallly affected by cerebellar
          damage?

     c.   Discuss the role of the cerebellum in controlling saccades.

d. Describe the motor control required to touch one's finger to one's nose as quickly as possible.

e. Why may a police officer use the finger-to-nose test to check for alcohol intoxication?

f. From what sources does the cerebellum receive input? To which structures do its output fibers project?

g. Describe the functions of the cerebellar cortex and the cerebellar nuclei.

h. Describe the relationship between the Purkinje cells and the parallel fibers. How does this affect movement?

3. *The role of the basal ganglia*
   a. What structures comprise the basal ganglia?

   b. Which are the main receptive areas? the main output area? Where does the sensory input come from, and where does the output go?

   c. How does cerebellar function compare with that of the basal ganglia?

4. *The role of the cerebral cortex*
   a. Contrast the roles of the spinal cord and primary motor cortex in the control of movement.

   b. Describe the roles of the prefrontal, premotor, and supplementary motor cortex.

c. What is a movement vector? Describe the experiment that suggested that monkeys could do a "mental rotation."

d. Where does the pyramidal system begin? Where is its first synapse? What is the source of its name?

e. From which structures does the extrapyramidal system originate? Describe the extrapyramidal side effects of certain drugs.

f. What is the relationship between the pyramidal system and the dorsolateral tract of the spinal cord? between the extrapyramidal system and the ventromedial tract?

g. Which movements are controlled by the dorsolateral tract, and which by the ventromedial tract?

Disorders of movement

1. *Myasthenia gravis*
   a. Describe the symptoms and cause of myasthenia gravis.

   b. What are two kinds of treatment for this disease?

2. *Parkinson's disease*
   a. Describe the symptoms and immediate cause of Parkinson's disease.

   b. How strong is the evidence for a genetic predisposition for Parkinson's disease?

   c. List the possible environmental factors in Parkinson's disease.

d. How did the experience with a heroin substitute lead to suspicion of an environmental toxin as a cause of this disease?

e. How may MPTP and paraquat be implicated?

f. Discuss the problems with the toxin-exposure hypothesis.

g. What is the rationale for treatment of Parkinson's disease with L-DOPA? What are the side effects of this treatment?

h. What is the rationale for the use of deprenyl to slow the progress of Parkinson's disease? Contrast the effects of deprenyl and of L-DOPA on Parkinson's disease.

i. How successful are current attempts to treat Parkinson's disease with brain grafts or genetically altered cells?

3. *Huntington's disease*
    a. What are the physical and psychological symptoms of Huntington's disease?

    b. Which neurons degenerate in Huntington's disease? What is a possible cause of the degeneration?

    c. Discuss the role of genetics in Huntington's disease.

    d. What do we know about the base sequence of the gene for Huntington's disease?

POSTTEST

Multiple-Choice Questions

1. Which of the following is true of nerves and muscles?
   a. There is a one-to-one relationship between axons and muscle fibers.
   b. Each axon innervates several or many muscle fibers.
   c. Each muscle fiber receives several or many axons.
   d. Each axon innervates many muscle fibers, and each muscle fiber receives many axons.

2. Acetylcholine
   a. has only excitatory effects on skeletal muscles.
   b. has excitatory effects on some skeletal muscles and inhibitory effects on others.
   c. has only inhibitory effects on skeletal muscles; norepinephrine has only excitatory effects on those muscles.
   d. is released only onto smooth muscles, never onto skeletal muscles.

3. Which of the following is a type of skeletal muscle?
   a. slow-twitch, white, fatigue-resistant
   b. fast-twitch, white, fatigue-resistant
   c. slow-twitch, pink, fatigue-prone
   d. slow-twitch, red, fatigue-resistant

4. The muscle spindle
   a. is a stretch receptor located in parallel to the muscle.
   b. inhibits the motor neuron innervating the muscle when it is stretched; this leads to relaxation of the muscle.
   c. responds only when the muscle contracts.
   d. synapses directly onto the muscle to excite it directly.

5. The Golgi tendon organ
   a. is also located in the muscle spindle.
   b. affects the motor neuron in the same way as the muscle spindle, thereby enhancing its effect.
   c. responds when the muscle contracts.
   d. excites the motor neuron that innervates the muscle.

6. Ballistic movements
   a. proceed automatically once triggered.
   b. require feedback as they are being executed.
   c. are controlled largely by the basal ganglia.
   d. are required when a singer holds a note for a long time.

7. An example of an oscillator is
   a. singing a prolonged note.
   b. contraction of the pupil.
   c. threading a needle.
   d. wing flapping in birds.

8. The rhythm of a dog's scratch reflex
   a. varies, though the length and strength of each scratching movement are constant.
   b. is constant at four to five scratches per second, though the length and strength of each scratch can vary.
   c. is an example of feedback control.
   d. is organized in the cerebellum.

9. Which of the following is true?
   a. Feedback control must be at the root of all movements; otherwise we would be unable to modify our behavior.
   b. Singing a single note does not require feedback, although singing several notes in a sequence does require feedback.
   c. Even ballistic movements are in reality feedback controlled.
   d. There are involuntary components of many voluntary behaviors.

10. Grooming behavior of mice
    a. is an example of a fixed action pattern.
    b. is an example of feedback-guided behavior.
    c. totally disappears if the mouse has no forelimbs to execute the main movements.
    d. can be observed as disorganized random elements of behavior if the mouse has no forelimbs to execute the main movements.

11. The motor program for scratching in cats
    a. requires feedback from muscle movements.
    b. is contained in the primary motor cortex.
    c. is contained in the spinal cord.
    d. varies in rate according to the intensity of the stimulus.

12. The cerebellum
    a. is large and critical for the behavior of sloths.
    b. is especially important for planning and coordination of complex, rapid movements.
    c. is important only for innate, not learned, motor responses.
    d. more than one of the above.

13. Damage to the cerebellum produces
    a. Parkinson's disease.
    b. Huntington's disease.
    c. deficits in saccadic movements of the eyes.
    d. deficits in slow feedback-controlled movements.

14. In executing the "finger-to-nose" movement quickly
    a. the cerebellar cortex is important in the initial rapid movement.
    b. the cerebellar nuclei are important in maintaining the brief hold pattern.
    c. other structures are important in the final slow movement.
    d. all of the above.

15. Purkinje cells in the cerebellum
    a. receive input from parallel fibers.
    b. send output to parallel fibers.
    c. excite cells in the cerebellar nuclei.
    d. send output to the basal ganglia and cerebral cortex.

16. The basal ganglia are important for
    a. rapid ballistic movements.
    b. planning and control of the distance and direction of postural movements.
    c. wing flapping in birds.
    d. fine control of movement.

17. The primary motor cortex
    a. provides the major motor output to the spinal cord.
    b. includes the somatomotor, prefrontal, premotor, and supplementary motor cortex, as well as the basal ganglia.
    c. is active before, but not during, a movement.
    d. all of the above.

18. The order of activity in preparing for and executing a movement is
    a. primary motor, premotor, prefrontal cortex.
    b. premotor, prefrontal, primary motor cortex.
    c. prefrontal, premotor, primary motor cortex.
    d. primary motor, prefrontal, premotor cortex.

19. A movement vector
    a. is a type of neuron in the primary motor cortex.
    b. is a type of neuron in the supplementary motor cortex.
    c. is a representation of the activity of a single neuron, which may produce movement in one direction at one time, and in another direction at another time.
    d. is a representation of the relative activity of a group of neurons, each of which has a preferred direction of movement.

20. The pyramidal system
    a. originates mostly in the primary motor cortex and adjacent areas.
    b. is responsible for control of gross postural adjustments.
    c. has many synapses between cortex and spinal motor neurons.
    d. all of the above.

21. Which of the following comprise the extrapyramidal system?
    a. the primary motor cortex and adjacent areas
    b. the cerebellum and dorsolateral tract of the spinal cord
    c. the dorsolateral and ventrolateral tracts of the spinal cord
    d. widespread parts of the cerebral cortex, the basal ganglia, cerebellum, red nucleus, and reticular formation

22. The pyramids of the medulla
    a. contain the cell bodies of the pyramidal system.
    b. contain the cell bodies of the extrapyramidal system.
    c. are the site where axons of the pyramidal system cross from one side to the other.
    d. are the site where axons of the extrapyramidal system cross from one side to the other.

23. The dorsolateral tract of the spinal cord
    a. contains crossed fibers of the pyramidal system and red nucleus.
    b. controls movements in the periphery of the body.
    c. controls movements on the side of the body opposite the brain area where the fibers originate.
    d. all of the above.

24. The ventromedial tract of the spinal cord
    a. contains crossed fibers of the pyramidal system and red nucleus.
    b. controls movements near the midline of the body that are necessarily bilateral.
    c. controls movements on the side of the body opposite the brain area where the fibers originate.
    d. is identical to the extrapyramidal system.

25. Myasthenia gravis
    a. probably results from destruction of acetylcholine receptors at neuromuscular junctions by an autoimmune process.
    b. is helped by drugs that increase the effect of acetylcholinesterase.
    c. is helped by drugs that enhance the function of the immune system.
    d. all of the above.

26. Parkinson's disease
    a. results from too much dopamine in the basal ganglia.
    b. results from too little acetylcholine at the neuromuscular junction.
    c. results from too little dopamine in the basal ganglia.
    d. can be cured by taking dopamine pills.

27. MPTP
    a. has been used with some success in treating Parkinson's disease.
    b. may be an environmental cause of Parkinson's disease.
    c. may be an environmental cause of myasthenia gravis.
    d. has been used with some success in treating myasthenia gravis.

28. Deprenyl
    a. blocks conversion of MPTP to MPP^+ by monoamine oxidase B.
    b. blocks conversion of paraquat to MPTP by monoamine oxidase B.
    c. decreases symptoms of Parkinson's disease but does not slow its progress.
    d. slows the progress of Huntington's disease.

29. Huntington's disease
    a. can be treated effectively with kainic acid or quinolinic acid.
    b. can be treated effectively with L-DOPA.
    c. can be treated with drugs that suppress the immune system.
    d. may result from overstimulation of neurons by glutamate or a similar chemical.

30. Huntington's disease
    a. results from destruction of dopaminergic input to the basal ganglia.
    b. is characterized by great weakness.
    c. is caused by a dominant gene on human chromosome number 4.
    d. is caused by a recessive gene on human chromosome number 10.

31. Which of the following are *not* symptoms of Huntington's disease?
   a. facial twitch and tremors
   b. depression and anxiety
   c. memory impairment and alcohol and drug abuse
   d. weakness and difficulty initiating movements

32. The gene associated with Huntington's disease
   a. in its normal form, contains a sequence of bases repeated 11 to 24 times.
   b. in its normal form, does not contain any repeated sequences of bases.
   c. is now known to be the code for acetylcholine receptors.
   d. is now known to be the code for tyrosine hydroxylase, which produces L-dopa from tyrosine.

Answers to Multiple-Choice Questions

1. b	9. d	17. a	25. a
2. a	10. a	18. c	26. c
3. d	11. c	19. d	27. b
4. a	12. b	20. a	28. a
5. c	13. c	21. d	29. d
6. a	14. d	22. c	30. c
7. d	15. a	23. d	31. d
8. b	16. b	24. b	32. a

Diagrams

1. Label the principal areas of the motor cortex in the human brain: posterior parietal cortex, prefrontal cortex, premotor cortex, primary motor cortex, primary somatosensory cortex, supplementary motor cortex.

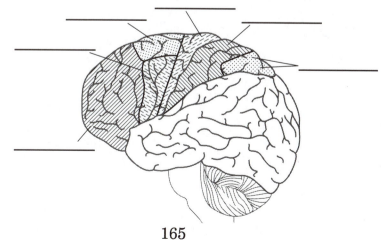

2. Label the following components of the basal ganglia: caudate nucleus, putamen, globus pallidus (lateral part), globus pallidus (medial part), thalamus, subthalamic nucleus, amygdala, substantia nigra.

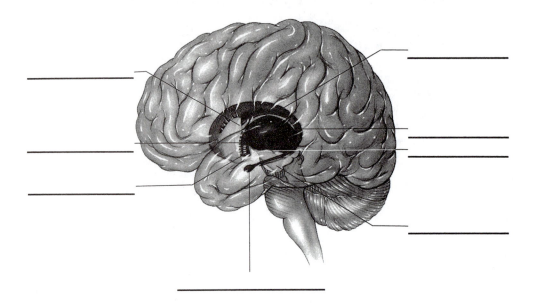

9

RHYTHMS OF WAKEFULNESS AND SLEEP

INTRODUCTION

All vertebrate species that have been studied exhibit endogenous rhythms of behavior. Circannual (approximately year-long) cycles govern hibernation, migration, and seasonal mating in some species. Virtually all vertebrates exhibit circadian (approximately 24-hour) cycles of activity and sleep as well as of other bodily functions. The "clock" governing these cycles generates the rhythm internally, although the external light cycles affect the specific settings. Light appears to act on the suprachiasmatic nucleus (SCN) of the hypothalamus. If the axons from the retina to the SCN are changed, light can no longer reset the biological clock, even though the individual can see. Whether or not light stimuli are available to reset the clock, it will continue to generate circadian rhythms. The mechanism of the clock is not understood, but it does not appear to depend on rhythms of breathing, heart rate, or neural activity.

The basic function of sleep is also ill defined. The main effect of sleep deprivation is an increasing urge to sleep, which is more intense at night. However, the urge to sleep seems out of proportion to the mild behavioral disorders that result from lack of sleep. The repair and restoration theory proposes that restorative functions occur mostly during sleep; however, this may be true only for the brain. The evolutionary theory proposes that sleep is basically an energy-conserving mechanism employed during times when activity would be either inefficient or dangerous. Elements of both these theories may be valid.

Relaxed wakefulness (with the eyes closed) is characterized by synchronized alpha waves (about 10 per second). The synchrony results from sources of inherent rhythmic activity in the brain that are not overridden by strong sensory input or mental effort. Stage 1 of sleep is signaled by desynchronized activity, after which progression through stages 2, 3, and 4 is correlated with increasingly slow and synchronized waves. Throughout the night, there is a cyclic progression back and forth through the four stages. However, after the first period of stage 1, each return to stage 1 is correlated with rapid eye movements, relaxed muscles, and rapid and variable heart rate and breathing. Rapid eye movement (REM) sleep has also been called paradoxical sleep, because the EEG waves are desynchronized as during wakefulness, but the person is harder to waken than during any other stage of sleep. As with sleep in general, the function of REM sleep is not well understood. However, dreams may result from the brain's attempt to make sense of its increased activity during REM episodes (activation-synthesis hypothesis). In general, the percentage of sleep spent in REM correlates positively with the total amount of sleep.

Alert wakefulness is characterized by desynchronized EEG activity, resulting from varied and multiple inputs to cortical neurons that cause them to fire out of phase with each other. Wakefulness and behavioral arousal depend on the ascending reticular activating system (ARAS). The ARAS is a group of large, branching neurons running through the hindbrain and midbrain. It receives input diffusely from all sensory systems and sends output equally diffusely to the cerebral cortex and other structures. It is poorly suited for processing specific sensory information but well designed to alert the whole brain to a change in the flow of sensory input.

Sleep does not result simply from a passive reduction of sensory input. A group of nuclei, called the raphe system, parallels the ARAS; early research suggested that this system, via its neurotransmitter serotonin, actively induces sleep. Damage to the raphe system results in a period of prolonged wakefulness, followed by a gradual return of reduced amounts of sleep. However, raphe neurons are more active during wakefulness than during sleep. Several areas of the hypothalamus, thalamus, and brain stem may cooperate to induce the onset of sleep. Prostaglandin D_2 and Factor S, both of which circulate in the blood, may increase sleepiness. Just before and during REM sleep, high-amplitude potentials can be recorded in the pons, geniculate, and occipital cortex (PGO waves); these waves are correlated with the rapid eye movements. Animals compensate for lost PGO waves more precisely than lost time in REM. Cells in the pons that release acetylcholine appear to initiate REM sleep.

There are three categories of insomnia: onset, maintenance, and termination. Causes of insomnia include abnormalities of biological rhythms, sleep apnea, overuse of sleeping pills, and periodic movements in sleep. Narcolepsy refers to periods of extreme sleepiness during the day. Additional symptoms of narcolepsy are cataplexy (extreme muscle weakness while awake), sleep paralysis (inability to move during transition into or out of sleep), and hypnagogic hallucinations (dreamlike experiences that are difficult to distinguish from reality). All of these symptoms can be interpreted as intrusions of REM sleep into wakefulness. Nightmares are unpleasant dreams that occur during REM sleep; night terrors are experiences of extreme anxiety, occurring during non-REM sleep. Sleep talking occurs with similar probability in REM and non-REM sleep, whereas sleepwalking occurs mostly during stages 3 and 4 slow-wave sleep. REM behavior disorder is a condition in which people act out their dreams; this probably results from damage to the areas of the pons and midbrain that normally inhibit motor neurons during REM sleep.

KEY TERMS AND CONCEPTS

The alternation of sleeping and waking
1. Endogenous cycles as a preparation for external changes
    Endogenous circannual and circadian rhythms
        Migratory restlessness
    Setting and resetting the cycle
        Biological clock
        Free-running rhythm
        Zeitgeber
    Attempts to alter the biological clock
        Cave experiments

2. Resetting the biological clock
    Jet lag
        Worse going east
    Shift work and night shifts
        Exposure to bright lights

3. Location and nature of the biological clock
    Interference with the biological clock
        Curt Richter
        Lack of effect of most procedures
    Role of the suprachiasmatic nucleus (SCN)
        Axons from optic tract
        Independence from pathways for pattern vision
        Disconnected SCN still generates rhythms
        Genetic mutation that produces 20-hour rhythm
            Transplantation of mutant SCN

4. The functions of sleep
    The repair and restoration theory of sleep
        Only brain needs sleep for restoration
        Effects of sleep deprivation
            Differences between human and animal experiments
    The evolutionary theory of the need for sleep
        Hibernation
        Energy conservation
        Time required for food search
        Safety from predators

Sleeping and dreaming
1. The stages of sleep
    Alpha waves: relaxed wakefulness
    Stage 1 sleep
        Desynchronized EEG

Theta waves
Stage 2 sleep
Sleep spindle
K-complex
Stages 3 and 4 slow-wave sleep
Synchronized EEG

2. Paradoxical, or REM, sleep
Characteristics
Desynchronized EEG
Most difficult to awaken
Rapid eye movements
Rapid and variable heart rate and breathing
Postural relaxation
Penile erection or vaginal moistening
Sleep cycles
90- to 100-minute cycles
Stages 3 and 4 predominant early in night
REM predominant late in night
REM sleep and dreaming
Dreams reported on 80 to 90% of awakenings from REM

3. The functions of REM sleep
Individual and species differences in REM sleep
Percent of time in REM correlated with length of sleep
The effects of REM sleep deprivation in humans
Increased anxiety and irritability
Decreased concentration
Increased appetite
REM rebound
The effects of paradoxical sleep deprivation in nonhumans
Impairments in learning

4. A biological perspective on dreaming
Activation-synthesis hypothesis
Paralysis of postural muscles

Brain mechanisms in sleep and its disorders
1. Wakefulness and the reticular activating system
Cerveau isolé: prolonged sleep
Not due to loss of sensory input
Ascending reticular activating system (ARAS)
Interconnected network
Multisynaptic pathways
Diffuse input and output

2. Physiological mechanisms of sleep and REM sleep
   Sleep-inducing areas
      Raphe system
         Damage: insomnia for a few days
         Serotonin depletion: insomnia for a few days
         More active during wakefulness
         May inhibit REM sleep
      Parts of hypothalamus, thalamus, brain stem
         Stimulation increases probability of sleep
         Damage decreases sleep
   The biochemistry of sleep
      Chemicals in blood
         Prostaglandin D_2: induces sleep, lowers temperature
         Factor S: induces slow-wave sleep
   REM-inducing areas
      PGO (pons-geniculate-occipital cortex) waves
   The biochemistry of REM sleep
      Pons cells that release acetylcholine
         Carbachol
      Pons cells that release glutamate
         Descending reticular formation
         Inhibition of motor neurons of spinal cord

3. Abnormalities of sleep
   Insomnia
      Onset insomnia
         Possible cause: phase-delayed temperature rhythm
      Maintenance insomnia
         Possible cause: circadian rhythm irregularity
      Termination insomnia
         Possible cause: phase-advanced temperature rhythm
         Early onset of REM sleep
   Sleep apnea
   Overuse of sleeping pills
      Withdrawal effects
      Advance or delay biological clock
   Periodic movements in sleep
   Narcolepsy
      Attacks of daytime sleepiness
      Cataplexy
      Sleep paralysis
      Hypnagogic hallucinations
      May be due to intrusion of REM into wakefulness
   Night terrors, sleep talking, sleepwalking
      Night terrors different from nightmares
         Occur in non-REM sleep

Sleep talking
    Occurs in REM or non-REM sleep
Sleepwalking
    Occurs mostly in stage 3 or 4 sleep
REM behavior disorder
  Acting out dreams
  Damage in pons and midbrain
    Motor neurons no longer inhibited by glycine

SHORT-ANSWER QUESTIONS

The alternation of sleep and waking

1. *Endogenous cycles as a preparation for external changes*
   a. What do we know about the factors that initiate migration in birds?

   b. What are endogenous circannual rhythms? endogenous circadian rhythms? How consistent are circadian rhythms?

   c. How can circadian rhythms be demonstrated experimentally? What are some bodily and behavioral changes that occur in circadian rhythms?

d. What is a Zeitgeber? What is the most effective Zeitgeber?

e. How easily can the biological clock be changed to a new cycle length?

2. *Resetting the biological clock*
    a. Is it easier to cross time zones going east or west? Why?

    b. What is the best way to reset the biological clock when working a night shift?

3. *Location and nature of the biological clock*
    a. What sorts of attempted interference with the biological clock were not effective?

b. What structure is the source of the circadian rhythms? What is its relationship to the visual system?

c. What is the evidence that the SCN generates rhythms itself?

d. What happened when the SCN from hamsters with a mutant gene for a 20-hour rhythm were transplanted to normal hamsters?

4. *The functions of sleep*
   a. Describe the repair and restoration theory of sleep. What evidence supports this theory? What are the problems with it?

   b. Describe the evolutionary theory of the need for sleep. What evidence supports it? What are its problems?

c. How compatible are these two theories?

Sleeping and dreaming
1. *The stages of sleep*
    a. Describe the usual behavioral correlate of alpha waves. What is the frequency of alpha waves?

    b. Describe the EEG in stage 1 sleep.

    c. What are the EEG characteristics of stage 2 sleep?

    d. Which stages of sleep are classed as slow-wave sleep (SWS)?

e. Why is EEG activity sometimes synchronized and sometimes desynchronized?

2. *Paradoxical, or REM, sleep*
   a. Why is REM sleep sometimes called paradoxical sleep? What are its characteristics?

   b. What is the typical duration of the sleep cycle? During which part of the night is REM predominant? During which part is stage 3 and 4 SWS predominant?

   c. How good is the correlation between REM and dreaming?

3. *The functions of REM sleep*
   a. What is the relationship between percentage of time in REM and total sleep time? How consistent is this relationship across species and across individuals within a species?

b. What kinds of behavioral changes occur if people are selectively deprived of REM sleep?

c. Describe the apparent relationship between learning and paradoxical sleep.

4. *A biological perspective on dreaming*
    a. What is the current view of Freud's assumptions concerning dreaming?

    b. State the activation-synthesis hypothesis. What evidence supports this hypothesis? How widely accepted is it?

Brain mechanisms in sleep and its disorders
1. *Wakefulness and the reticular activating system*
    a. What brain structure is especially important in controlling wakefulness and arousal?

b. What is a cerveau isolé preparation? What is the result of such a cut? Was this result due simply to loss of sensory input?

c. Describe the input, output, and interconnections of the ARAS.

2. *Physiological mechanisms of sleep and REM sleep*
   a. What evidence implicated the raphe system as a major sleep-inducing area of the brain? What is the major transmitter of this system?

   b. What are the problems with the hypothesis that the raphe system is the major sleep-inducing area?

   c. What other areas seem to contribute to sleep onset?

d. What blood-borne chemicals may promote sleep?

e. What are PGO waves? Where are they recorded? What is their relationship to rapid eye movements?

f. What happens to PGO waves during and immediately after a period of REM deprivation?

g. Which neurotransmitter is released by cells in the pons that trigger REM sleep? Which drug can elicit REM sleep if injected into the pons?

h. Describe the mechanism for inhibiting motor activity during REM sleep.

3. *Abnormalities of sleep*
   a. List and describe the characteristics of the three categories of insomnia. What circadian rhythm disorders may cause each category?

   b. Describe the symptoms of sleep apnea. What is one cause of sleep apnea?

   c. What are the pharmacological effects of most tranquilizers that are used as sleeping pills? How are midazolam and triazolam different from other types of sleeping pill.

   d. What are three ways in which sleeping pills may contribute to insomnia?

   e. Describe the symptoms of periodic movements in sleep.

f.   What four symptoms are commonly associated with narcolepsy?

g.   Define cataplexy. What tends to trigger it? Define hypnagogic
     hallucinations.

h.   What is a likely cause of narcolepsy?

i.   How do night terrors differ from nightmares? During which
     type of sleep are night terrors most common?

j.   During which stages does sleep talking occur? sleepwalking?

k.   What are the symptoms and possible cause of REM behavior disorder?

POSTTEST

Multiple-Choice Questions

1. Curt Richter suggested the revolutionary idea that
    a.   nearly all behavior is a reaction to a stimulus.
    b.   the body generates its own cycles of activity and inactivity.
    c.   temperature fluctuations are the best zeitgeber.
    d.   animals wait till the first frost before preparing for winter so that they can enjoy summer longer.

2. Migratory birds
    a.   respond only to temperature signals to begin migration.
    b.   respond only to the ratio of light to dark, especially in spring.
    c.   respond only to the availability of food.
    d.   show migratory restlessness every spring and fall, even in captivity with constant light/dark cycles.

3. Circadian rhythms
    a.   cannot be demonstrated if lights are always on or always off.
    b.   always average within a minute or two of 24 hours in length, regardless of the light cycle.
    c.   include cycles of body activity, temperature, and urine production.
    d.   are very flexible and can be changed as soon as a different light cycle is established.

4. Which of the following is true?
    a.   It is easier to adjust our biological rhythms to longer cycles and to travel across time zones going west.
    b.   It is easier to adjust our biological rhythms to shorter cycles and to travel across time zones going east.
    c.   People on night shifts tend to sleep the longest when they get to sleep very late at night or early in the morning.
    d.   People on night shifts that were exposed to normal levels of room lighting (about 150 lux) found it easy to adjust their cycles.

5. Which of the following can totally disrupt the biological clock?
   a. food or water deprivation
   b. anesthesia
   c. long periods of forced activity or forced inactivity
   d. none of the above

6. The suprachiasmatic nucleus
   a. is located in the brain stem.
   b. depends on the same processing as patterned vision
   c. is concerned only with the resetting of the clock, not with generating the rhythm.
   d. if transplanted from fetal hamsters that have a mutant gene producing a 20-hour cycle, into normal hamsters, will produce 20-hour cycles in the recipients.

7. When people are deprived of sleep for a week or more
   a. some report dizziness, irritability, and difficulty concentrating, but no drastic consequences.
   b. usually suffer severe consequences, including death.
   c. processes such as digestion, removal of waste products, and protein synthesis are greatly slowed.
   d. they report no symptoms whatever.

8. The evolutionary theory of sleep
   a. states that species regulate their sleep time according to how much repair and restoration their bodies need.
   b. states that species evolved a mechanism to promote energy conservation at times when they are relatively inefficient.
   c. is incompatible with other theories concerning repair and restoration.
   d. is currently very well established.

9. Alpha waves are characteristic of
   a. REM sleep.
   b. alert mental activity.
   c. relaxed wakefulness.
   d. slow-wave sleep.

10. Desynchronized EEG activity is seen
    a. during slow-wave sleep.
    b. when a great deal of input to the cerebral cortex excites and inhibits neurons out of phase with each other.
    c. when there is little input to the brain and firing rate is slow.
    d. when neurons are all doing the same thing at the same time.

11. Which of the following is *not* a sign of REM sleep?
    a. ease of awakening
    b. relatively fast, variable heart and breathing rates
    c. extreme relaxation of large muscles
    d. desynchronized EEG activity

12. Paradoxical sleep is paradoxical because brain waves signify
    a. slow-wave sleep, when one is really dreaming.
    b. dreaming, when one is really in slow-wave sleep.
    c. sleep, when one is really awake.
    d. wakefulness, when one is behaviorally deeply asleep.

13. Dreams
    a. are highly correlated with sleep talking.
    b. are of greater duration and frequency during the early part of the night.
    c. are correlated highly, but not perfectly, with periods of REM sleep, even in those who claim not to dream.
    d. all of the above.

14. After about a week of REM deprivation, at least some subjects
    a. reported increased anxiety, irritability and impaired concentration.
    b. experienced increased appetite and weight gain.
    c. spent somewhat more sleep time on subsequent nights in REM sleep.
    d. all of the above.

15. Comparisons of sleep patterns across individuals and across species indicate that
    a. percentage of time spent in REM increases as total amount of sleep increases.
    b. percentage of time in REM decreases as total amount of sleep increases.
    c. percentage of time in REM remains the same, no matter how long the individual sleeps.
    d. percentage of time spent in REM is extremely variable, and shows no relationship to the total amount of sleep.

16. The activation-synthesis hypothesis proposes that dreams result from
    a. unconscious wishes struggling for expression.
    b. the ego's attempt to gain control of the id.
    c. the brain's attempt to make sense of its activity.
    d. the brain's attempt to wake up.

17. A cut through the midbrain (cerveau isolé)
    a. left the animal sleeping constantly because most sensory input was cut off from the brain.
    b. produced prolonged sleep because an area that promotes wakefulness was cut off from the rest of the brain.
    c. left the animal sleeping and waking normally, since structures that control these functions are anterior to the hindbrain.
    d. left the animal more wakeful than usual because much of the ARAS was still connected to the brain but a sleep-promoting system had been damaged.

18. The ARAS
    a. is very discretely organized, with few interconnections.
    b. is important in generating slow-wave sleep.
    c. is primarily concerned with sensory analysis.
    d. none of the above.

19. Damage to the raphe system results in
    a. total and permanent sleep.
    b. total and permanent wakefulness.
    c. a period of prolonged wakefulness followed by a partial return of sleep.
    d. constant slow-wave sleep without any REM.

20. Prostaglandin D_2 and Factor S
    a. are blood-borne chemicals that promote sleepiness.
    b. are neurotransmitters that induce REM sleep.
    c. are neurotransmitters that promote wakefulness.
    d. are blood-borne chemicals that block REM sleep.

21. REM sleep occurs
    a. only early in a night's sleep.
    b. cyclically, about every 90 minutes.
    c. randomly throughout the night.
    d. only after a period of physical exercise.

22. PGO waves
    a. are synchronized with rapid eye movements.
    b. are recorded in the pons, lateral geniculate, and occipital cortex.
    c. are compensated more completely than total REM time, if "lost" due to REM deprivation.
    d. all of the above.

23. Neurons that are more active just before and during REM are located in
    a. the ARAS.
    b. the raphe system.
    c. the pons.
    d. all of the above.

24. Chemical depletion of serotonin would produce generally the same effects on sleep patterns as lesions of
    a. REM-inducing part of the pons.
    b. raphe system.
    c. ARAS.
    d. suprachiasmatic nucleus.

25. Acetylcholine appears to
    a. promote REM sleep.
    b. inhibit slow-wave sleep.
    c. inhibit REM sleep.
    d. promote slow-wave sleep.

26. People with phase-delayed temperature rhythms who try to fall asleep at the normal time may experience
    a. onset insomnia.
    b. maintenance insomnia.
    c. termination insomnia.
    d. excess sleep.

27. Which of the following is a cause of insomnia?
    a. narcolepsy
    b. cataplexy
    c. sleep apnea
    d. hypnagogic hallucinations

28. Which of the following is true of sleeping pills?
    a. They are the best treatment for jet lag.
    b. Short-acting ones may cause a person to awaken too early and be unable to get back to sleep.
    c. They are generally harmless remedies for insomnia.
    d. They are the major cause of REM behavior disorder.

29. Which of the following is associated primarily with REM sleep?
    a. nightmares
    b. night terrors
    c. sleep talking
    d. all of the above

Answers to Multiple-Choice Questions

1. b	7. a	13. c	19. c	25. a
2. d	8. b	14. d	20. a	26. a
3. c	9. c	15. a	21. b	27. c
4. a	10. b	16. c	22. d	28. b
5. d	11. a	17. b	23. c	29. a
6. d	12. d	18. d	24. b	

Diagram

Label the following parts of the sleep/wakefulness system: cerebral cortex, medulla, pons, raphe system, ascending reticular activating system. Lines a and b indicate cuts through the brain stem. Which cut produces increased wakefulness? Which produces increased somnolence?

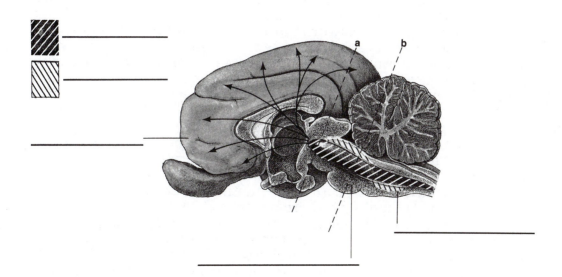

10

THE REGULATION OF
INTERNAL BODY STATES

INTRODUCTION

Homeostatic drives are drives that tend to maintain certain biological conditions within a fixed range. Temperature regulation in mammals and birds is such a drive. Constant relatively high temperatures provide conditions in which chemical reactions can be regulated precisely and, by increasing the metabolic rate, increase capacity for prolonged activity. Several physiological mechanisms, including shivering, sweating, panting, and redirection of blood flow, raise and lower temperature appropriately. These are coordinated primarily by the preoptic area, which monitors both its own temperature and that of the skin and spinal cord. Behavioral regulation of temperature is used both by animals that are poikilothermic (body temperature matches that of environment) and by those that are homeothermic (body temperature is regulated within a few degrees of a constant setting). The preoptic area, the posterior hypothalamus, and other areas are important for behavioral temperature regulation. Fever is produced when leukocytes (white blood cells) release interleukin-1, which causes production of prostaglandin E_1, which in turn causes the preoptic area to raise body temperature. Moderate fevers are helpful in combating bacterial infections. Body temperature of infant animals is an important influence on their behaviors.

Water balance is critical, both for regulating the concentration of chemicals in our bodily fluids (and therefore the rate of chemical reactions) and for maintaining normal blood pressure. If we have ample supplies of palatable fluids to drink, we may drink a great deal of them and let the kidneys discard the excess. If there is a shortage of fluids to drink, or a large loss of water, the posterior pituitary releases vasopressin (also known as antidiuretic hormone, or ADH), which increases water retention by the kidneys. There are two major types of stimuli for thirst: decreased water content inside cells and decreased blood volume. When water is lost from the body, or when there are increased solutes in the blood, the blood becomes more concentrated. Water tends to flow out of cells into the area of higher osmotic pressure (blood). The resulting loss of water from cells in the OVLT (organum vasculosum laminae terminalis) elicits neural responses that are relayed to several hypothalamic nuclei, including the supraoptic and paraventricular nuclei, which produce vasopressin, the hormone that is released from the posterior pituitary and that increases blood pressure and urine concentration. The OVLT also relays information to the lateral preoptic area, which gives rise to osmotic thirst. Thus, an increase in osmotic signals results in greater water retention, increased water intake, and higher blood pressure. If large amounts of whole blood are lost, the resulting hypovolemia (low volume of blood) is detected by baroreceptors in the large veins; these receptors send information to areas in the hypothalamus that increase drinking. Baroreceptors in the kidney also detect the hypovolemia. The kidney then releases renin, which acts in the blood to produce angiotensin II. This hormone causes constriction of blood vessels to maintain blood pressure. It also stimulates neurons in the subfornical organ, which in turn relay the signal to neurons in the preoptic area, which produces hypovolemic thirst. The signals from the baroreceptors and angiotensin are synergistic.

Loss of sodium and other solutes results in an immediate and automatic craving for sodium. This sodium hunger depends largely on two hormones, aldosterone and angiotensin II. Aldosterone, secreted by the adrenal glands, causes the kidneys to conserve sodium and stimulates the OVLT and other areas around the third ventricle to increase salt intake. Angiotensin II, as noted above, stimulates the subfornical area to induce drinking; it also stimulates the medial amygdala to produce sodium hunger. The effects of aldosterone and angiotensin II are strongly synergistic.

The factors regulating hunger, satiety, and the selection of specific foods are very complex. Food selection is influenced by the digestive system (including intestinal enzymes), cultural factors, taste, familiarity, and memories of the consequences of consuming a particular food. Hunger and satiety depend on stimuli from the mouth, stomach, and duodenum, as well as blood glucose levels, metabolic rate, and food-specific stimuli. Damage to the lateral hypothalamus results in self-starvation, unless the animal is force-fed. The intact lateral hypothalamus contributes to feeding by modifying activity in the nucleus of the tractus solitarius (NTS), which may influence taste sensations and salivation, and also by increasing the release of digestive juices and of insulin, which promotes storage of circulating glucose. In addition, fibers passing through the lateral hypothalamus contribute to general arousal. Damage to the ventromedial hypothalamus results in obesity. This results from faster emptying of the stomach and increased release of insulin, which promotes fat storage and inhibits its release for use as fuel. As a result, the animal consumes more frequent meals. Damage to the paraventricular nucleus (PVN) also results in overeating. However, rats with PVN damage eat larger meals, rather than more frequent meals. Stimulation of the PVN by either serotonin or cholecystokinin (CCK) greatly decreases intake, especially of carbohydrates. Inhibition of the PVN by norepinephrine increases carbohydrate intake, and inhibition by neuropeptide Y or polypeptide YY also greatly increases meal size and promotes fat storage. The PVN may also affect food selection. Either norepinephrine or the hormone corticosterone injected into the PVN increases carbohydrate intake, whereas injection of the hormone aldosterone or the neurotransmitter galanin increases fat intake. Microdialysis experiments have shown that norepinephrine is released in the PVN mostly at the start of a meal (increasing carbohydrate intake), and serotonin is released primarily at the end (decreasing carbohydrate intake). Therefore, regulation of eating depends on a balance of neurotransmitters and hormones.

KEY TERMS AND CONCEPTS

Temperature regulation
1. Homeostasis
    Set range
    Set point

2. Mechanisms of controlling body temperature
    Poikilothermic
    Homeothermic
    Brain mechanisms of temperature regulation
        Hypothalamus
        Preoptic area
            Monitors own temperature
            Monitors temperature of skin and spinal cord
    Behavioral mechanisms of temperature regulation
        Preoptic area
        Posterior hypothalamus
        Other brain areas
    Fever
        Leukocytes
            Interleukin-1
            Prostaglandin E_1
        Preoptic area

3. Temperature regulation and behavior
    Body temperature and the development of animal behavior
        Requirement for warm temperature to show behavior
        "Distress calls"
            Thermoneutral zone
            Anthropomorphism
    Tonic immobility resonse

Thirst
1. Mechanisms of maintaining water balance
    Increasing intake
    Decreasing output
        Vasopressin or antidiuretic hormone (ADH)

2. The multiple causes of drinking
    Dry throat: minor signal
    Drinking with meals
    Taste and socialization

3. Osmotic thirst
    Osmotic pressure
    Semipermeable membrane
    Increase in solute concentration
        Water leaves cells
        Cells shrink
    Brain areas
        OVLT (organum vasculosum laminae terminalis)
        Supraoptic nucleus
        Paraventricular nucleus
        Lateral preoptic area
    Satisfied best by pure water (not salt water)

4. Hypovolemic thirst
    Polyethylene glycol
    Loss of blood volume
    Satisfied best by salt water
    Mechanisms of hypovolemic thirst
        Baroreceptors
        Hormones from kidneys
            Renin
            Angiotensinogen in blood
            Angiotensin II
        Subfornical organ
        Preoptic area
        Synergistic effects
    Sodium-specific cravings
        Automatic preference (not learned)
        Aldosterone
            Increased sodium retention by kidney
            Increased salt craving
        Angiotensin II
            Some brain areas: only thirst
            Medial amygdala: sodium hunger

Hunger
1. The digestive system and food selection
    Mouth
        Saliva
        Carbohydrate digestion

191

Stomach
    Hydrochloric acid
    Enzymes for protein digestion
Small intestine
    Protein, fat, and carbohydrate digestion
    Absorption
Large intestine
    Water and mineral absorption
    Lubrication
Digestive system influences on food selection
    Lactose, milk sugar
    Lactase enzyme
Other influences on food selection
    Carnivore
    Herbivore
    Omnivore
    Culture
    Taste
    Familiarity
    Learning

2.   Physiological mechanisms of hunger and satiety
    Oral factors
        Desire to taste or chew
        Fifth cranial nerve (trigeminal)
        Sham feeding
    Stomach stimulation
        Vagus nerve (cranial nerve 10)
            Information about stretching of stomach
        Splanchnic nerves
            Information about nutrient contents
    The duodenum and the hormone CCK
        CCK (cholecystokinin)
            Inhibits stomach emptying
    Blood glucose
        Availability of all types of nutrients
        Insulin: facilitates glucose entry into cells
        Glucagon: liver releases glucose
    Metabolic rate
    Food-specific mechanisms of satiety

3.   Brain mechanisms of eating and weight control
    The lateral hypothalamus
        Lesions: starvation or weight loss
        Electrical stimulation: eating

Neurons vs. dopamine axons passing through
        Damage to dopamine axons with 6-OHDA: loss of arousal
        Damage to cell bodies: loss of feeding
    Regulation of taste, insulin release, and digestive juices
        NTS (nucleus of the tractus solitarius in pons)
        Forebrain structures that facilitate ingestion
        Stimulation of secretion of insulin and digestive juices
Medial areas of the hypothalamus
    Lesions: weight gain
    Ventromedial hypothalamic syndrome
        Ventral noradrenergic bundle
        Finickiness
        More meals per day
        Increased stomach motility and secretions
        Faster stomach emptying
        Increased insulin and fat storage
    Paraventricular nucleus
        Critical for ending meals
            Serotonin or CCK: decreased carbohydrate intake
            Norepinephrine: increased carbohydrate intake
            Neuropeptide Y or polypeptide YY: increased meal size
            and fat storage
        Diet selection
            Norepinephrine or corticosterone: increase
            carbohydrate
            Aldosterone or galanin: increase fat
Eating and neurotransmitters
    Microdialysis
        Norepinephrine in paraventricular nucleus at beginning of
        meal
        Serotonin in paraventricular nucleus at end of meal
    Size and frequency of meals: balance among neurotransmitters
    and hormones

4. Integration of multiple mechanisms

SHORT-ANSWER QUESTIONS

Temperature regulation
1. *Homeostasis*
    a. What is a homeostatic process?

b. What are some of the physiological processes that are controlled near a set point? What are some homeostatic processes that anticipate future needs?

c. Why does the scrotum of most male mammals hang outside the body? Why should pregnant women avoid hot baths?

2. *Mechanisms of controlling body temperature*
   a. Define the terms poikilothermic and homeothermic.

b. What are two advantages of a constant body temperature?

c. What two kinds of stimuli does the preoptic area monitor for temperature control?

d. What prevents the temperature of fish, amphibians, and reptiles from fluctuating wildly?

e. Describe the temperature regulation of infant rats and of mammals with damage to the preoptic area? What brain area, besides the preoptic area, is important for behavioral temperature regulation?

f. What is prostaglandin E_1, and what is its role in producing a fever?

g. Of what benefit is a fever?

3. *Temperature regulation and behavior*
    a. What was the key to eliciting behaviors such as odor conditioning and female sexual behavior in baby rats?

b. Why do infant rats emit vocalizations when they wander out of the nest? What effect do these vocalizations have on the mother rat?

c. Describe the tonic immobility response of baby birds. What is the major stimulus governing immobility?

Thirst
1. *Mechanisms of maintaining water balance*
   a. Describe the different mechanisms of maintaining water balance that have been developed by desert animals and by animals with an abundant water supply.

   b. What are the two functions of vasopressin when body fluids are low? What is its other name?

2. *The multiple causes of drinking*
   a. How important is a dry throat in inducing thirst?

3. *Osmotic thirst*
    a. What is osmotic pressure?

    b. How does the body "know" when its osmotic pressure is low?

    c. What are the roles of the OVLT, the supraoptic and paraventricular nuclei of the hypothalamus, and the lateral preoptic area?

    d. What does a normal animal do if a concentrated salt solution is injected into its blood? How does a normal animal respond to such an injection if its drinking water tastes bad? What is the response of an animal with damage to the lateral preoptic area?

4. *Hypovolemic thirst*
    a. Why is hypovolemia dangerous?

b.   Under what circumstances does hypovolemic thirst occur naturally? How may it be induced experimentally?

c.   Will an animal with hypovolemic thirst drink more pure water or more salt water with the same concentration as blood? Why?

d.   What is the role of baroreceptors in hypovolemic thirst?

e.   Describe the steps leading to the production of antiotensin II. What are its two main effects?

f.   Which brain structures seem to mediate hypovolemic thirst?

g. How may the effects of angiotensin II be enhanced?

h. What two effects of aldosterone are beneficial in cases of sodium deficiency? What other hormone contributes to salt hunger?

Hunger
1. *The digestive system and food selection*
   a. Enzymes for the digestion of what type of nutrient(s) are present in saliva? in the stomach? in the small intestine?

   b. From which structure is digested food absorbed?

   c. Why do newborn mammals stop nursing as they grow older?

d. Discuss the evidence that humans are a partial exception to the principle of lactose intolerance in adults.

e. List the factors that may influence food selection.

2. *Physiological mechanisms of hunger and satiety*
   a. What stimulus signals baby rat pups to stop drinking milk?

   b. Summarize the evidence for the importance of oral factors in hunger and satiety. What is the evidence that these factors are not sufficient to end a meal normally?

   c. How did Deutsch et al. demonstrate the importance of stomach distention in regulating meal size?

d. Which two nerves convey the stomach's satiety signals?

e. What is CCK? What is the likely mechanism by which it induces satiety?

f. Summarize the evidence for and against the importance of blood glucose in the regulation of appetite.

g. What is the effect of insulin on blood glucose? How does this affect hunger? Compare the effects of glucagon with those of insulin..

h. Why do people with untreated diabetes eat a lot but gain little weight? How is this similar to, and how is it different from, the effects of high levels of insulin?

i.   Discuss the role of basal metabolic rate in weight regulation.
     Why is it difficult to lose more than a few pounds?

3. *Brain mechanisms of eating and weight control*
    a.   Describe the evidence that led to the concept of the lateral
         hypothalamus as a hunger center.

    b.   What is 6-hydroxydopamine? What kind of neuronal damage
         does it inflict when injected into the lateral hypothalamus?
         What are the behavioral results of such damage?

    c.   What is the result of damage to lateral hypothalamic cell bodies?

    d.   By what three mechanisms may the lateral hypothalamus
         contribute to feeding?

e. Describe the various behavioral changes produced by lesions of the ventromedial hypothalamus, ventral noradrenergic bundle, and surrounding areas. Can we say that animals with such lesions show an overall increase in hunger or a lack of satiety?

f. To what factors can we attribute the obesity induced by ventromedial hypothalamus lesions?

g. What are the effects of damage to the paraventricular nucleus (PVN)? How are these effects different from those of ventromedial hypothalamus damage?

h. What are the effects of injecting serotonin or CCK into the PVN?

i. What are the effects of injecting norepinephrine into the PVN? neuropeptide Y or polypeptide YY?

j.   What is a possible link of polypeptide YY with a human eating disorder?

k.   How may two neurotransmitters and two hormones, acting in the PVN, influence diet selection?

l.   What is microdialysis? At what times, relative to meals, are norepinephrine and serotonin released in the PVN?

POSTTEST

Multiple-Choice Questions

1. Temperature regulation
    a.   is an example of a homeostatic mechanism.
    b.   is important for precise coordination of chemical reactions in the body.
    c.   is important in mammals and birds for increasing resting metabolic rate and, thereby, capacity for prolonged activity.
    d.   all of the above.

2. The preoptic area monitors
    a.   only its own temperature.
    b.   only skin and spinal cord temperature.
    c.   both its own and skin and spinal cord temperature.
    d.   the temperature of internal organs via nerve input from those organs.

3. Behavioral means of temperature regulation
   a. are the only means of temperature regulation in poikilotherms.
   b. are the only means of temperature regulation in homeotherms.
   c. do not become functional until adulthood.
   d. are regulated entirely by the preoptic area.

4. Fever
   a. is harmful and should always be reduced with aspirin.
   b. is produced primarily by prostaglandin E_1 acting on cells in the preoptic area.
   c. is produced directly by bacteria acting on the preoptic area.
   d. is especially high in baby rabbits, in response to infections.

5. Which of the following is true?
   a. Infant rats, in the first week of life, can exhibit odor conditioning and female sexual behavior, but only if tested at normal room temperature (20°-23°C).
   b. In the process of trying to stabilize its temperature, a baby rat exhales vigorously and accidentally produces "distress calls."
   c. Chicks, when grabbed by a predator, will feign death for many hours, because the predator's warmth keeps the chick warm enough so that it does not have to move around.
   d. All of the above are true.

6. Vasopressin
   a. raises blood pressure by constricting blood vessels.
   b. is also known as antidiuretic hormone, because it promotes water retention by the kidney.
   c. is secreted from the posterior pituitary, as a result of control by the supraoptic and paraventricular nuclei of the hypothalamus.
   d. all of the above.

7. The main reason that a salty meal makes us thirsty is that
   a. the salt carried in the blood produces cellular dehydration; such dehydration of cells in the OVLT results in osmotic thirst.
   b. the increased salt in the blood causes the liquid portion of the blood to enter OVLT cells, thus distending them and resulting in osmotic thirst.
   c. the increased salt in the blood causes the liquid portion of the blood to enter cells throughout the body, thereby inducing hypovolemia.
   d. the salt enters cells in the OVLT and stimulates them directly.

8. Lesions of the lateral preoptic area
   a. disrupt the control of hypovolemic, but not osmotic, thirst.
   b. result in increased drinking and decreased water retention by the kidney.
   c. result in decreased drinking and increased water retention by the kidney.
   d. primarily disrupt signals concerning the state of dryness of the throat.

9. Hypovolemic thirst
   a. can be induced by injections of concentrated salt solution.
   b. can be induced by injections of polyethylene glycol under the skin.
   c. is a result of low volume of water within the cells.
   d. none of the above.

10. After its blood volume has been reduced, an animal
    a. will drink more pure water than salt water of the same concentration as blood.
    b. will drink more salt water of the same concentration as blood than pure water.
    c. will not drink any more than usual, since both liquid and solute have been removed.
    d. will drink only highly concentrated salt water.

11. Angiotensin II
    a. is secreted by the kidney.
    b. causes water to leave cells in the preoptic area and thereby stimulates osmotic thirst.
    c. stimulates the subfornical organ, which relays the information to the preoptic area, which in turn can induce drinking.
    d. all of the above.

12. Which of the following is *not* likely to induce drinking?
    a. application of angiotensin II to the OVLT
    b. application of angiotensin II to the subfornical organ
    c. low blood pressure signals from baroreceptors in the large veins
    d. sodium chloride injections into blood

13. Salt craving
    a. develops automatically, without learning, when sodium intake is low.
    b. depends to a large extent on aldosterone secreted by the adrenal glands.
    c. is enhanced by angiotensin II in the medial amygdala
    d. all of the above.

14. In the stomach
    a. food is mixed with hydrochloric acid and enzymes for the digestion of protein.
    b. food is mixed with hydrochloric acid and enzymes for the digestion of carbohydrates.
    c. food is mixed with enzymes that aid the digestion of fats.
    d. absorption of food through the walls of the stomach occurs.

15. Lactase
    a. is the sugar in milk.
    b. is an intestinal enzyme for the digestion of milk.
    c. is abundant in almost all adult humans, but is lacking in adults of other mammalian species.
    d. is abundant in birds and reptiles, but is lacking in mammals.

16. Oral factors
    a. contribute to satiety but are not sufficient to determine the amount of food consumed.
    b. are irrelevant to satiety.
    c. are the single most important factor in inducing satiety.
    d. include only the taste of food.

17. If a cuff closes the outlet from the stomach to the small intestine
    a. the animal will not eat because of the trauma of the cuff.
    b. the animal will continue eating indefinitely, since food must pass beyond the stomach to trigger satiety.
    c. the animal will eat a normal-sized meal and stop.
    d. the animal will eat a normal meal, wait for it to be absorbed through the walls of the stomach, and then eat again.

18. Splanchnic nerves
    a. carry information about the nutrient contents of the stomach.
    b. carry information about the stretching of the stomach walls.
    c. are stimulated directly by cholecystokinin (CCK).
    d. secrete CCK into the circulatory system.

19. CCK
    a. is produced by the duodenum in response to the presence of food there.
    b. if administered before a meal, reduces the size of that meal.
    c. in large enough doses, can elicit a sequence of grooming and resting in rats, similar to their behavior after a meal.
    d. all of the above.

20. CCK exerts its effects primarily by
    a. making the animal nauseated.
    b. crossing the blood-brain barrier and binding to receptors in the brain.
    c. delaying further emptying of the stomach, thus magnifying the satiety-producing effect of food in the stomach.
    d. altering the release of insulin.

21. Glucose levels in the blood
    a. vary greatly and are closely monitored by neurons in the hypothalamus, thereby controlling hunger.
    b. may be a contributing factor in hunger motivation, but not the only one.
    c. are irrelevant as hunger signals.
    d. are elevated by insulin.

22. Insulin
    a. promotes entry of glucose into cells.
    b. is released by the liver.
    c. is no longer secreted after VMH lesions.
    d. is secreted in response to low blood sugar.

23. People with untreated diabetes eat more food because
    a. the vagus and splanchnic nerves are damaged.
    b. they excrete most of their glucose unused.
    c. they store too much of their glucose, so it is unavailable for use.
    d. their basal metabolic rate is too high.

24. Glucagon
    a. is high in the late autumn in migratory and hibernating species.
    b. is produced by the small intestine.
    c. stimulates the liver to convert glucose to glycogen for storage.
    d. stimulates the liver to convert stored glycogen to glucose for release into the blood.

25. Basal metabolic rate
    a. is increased when people diet, in order to generate more heat.
    b. is influenced almost exclusively by what we eat; genetic influence is minimal.
    c. uses more calories than does regular exercise.
    d. is virtually identical in all people.

26. Which of the following is true of lateral hypothalamic damage?
    a. It results in chronic inactivity and decreased responsiveness to sensory stimuli.
    b. At least some of the results are due to damage to axons passing through the area, rather than to cell bodies located there.
    c. At least some of the effects on eating are due to low levels of insulin and digestive juices.
    d. All of the above are true.

27. Obesity resulting from damage to the ventromedial hypothalamus and ventral noradrenergic bundle
    a. can be prevented by allowing the animals to eat only the same amount that they ate before the lesion.
    b. occurs because the stomach empties faster than normal and because insulin secretion is increased.
    c. results from a dramatic increase in the palability of all foods, resulting in overeating even of bitter or untasty food.
    d. results from eating much larger meals than usual, because of lack of satiety.

28. Which of the following is true of the paraventricular nucleus (PVN)?
    a. It is important for both ending a meal and diet selection.
    b. CCK or serotonin in the PVN increase carbohydrate intake.
    c. Neuropeptide Y or polypeptide YY in the PVN decrease fat intake.
    d. Aldosterone or galanin in the PVN primarily increase carbohydrate intake.

29. Microdialysis
    a. is a technique used primarily for damaging axons while leaving cell bodies intact.
    b. is a technique used primarily for damaging cell bodies while leaving axons intact.
    c. has been used to demonstrate that the PVN releases norepinephrine at the start of a meal and serotonin at the end of a meal.
    d. has been used to demonstrate that the PVN releases serotonin at the start of a meal and norepinephrine at the end of a meal.

Answers to Multiple-Choice Questions

1. d	7. a	13. d	19. d	25. c
2. c	8. c	14. a	20. c	26. d
3. a	9. b	15. b	21. b	27. b
4. b	10. b	16. a	22. a	28. a
5. b	11. c	17. c	23. b	29. c
6. d	12. a	18. a	24. d	

Diagram

Label the following areas: preoptic area, posterior hypothalamus, lateral hypothalamus, ventromedial hypothalamus, paraventricular nucleus of the hypothalamus.

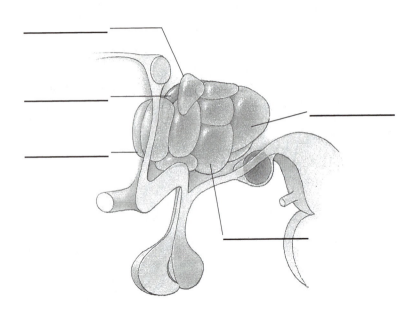

11

HORMONES AND
SEXUAL BEHAVIOR

INTRODUCTION

Hormones are released from various organs into the blood, which carries them throughout the body. Hormonal actions have slower onsets, longer times of action, and more diffuse effects than neural actions. There are several types of hormones. Protein and peptide hormones attach to receptors on the surface of cells, where they activate a second messenger, which in turn activates a series of enzymes. Steroid hormones attach to cytoplasmic receptors and move to the nucleus to alter gene expression. They may also have rapid effects on ion channels in the cell membrane. Two major classes of steroid hormones are androgens, which are more abundant in males, and estrogens, which are more abundant in females. Additional classes of hormones include thyroid hormones, monoamines, and others that are difficult to classify.

Most endocrine glands are regulated by the pituitary, which in turn is controlled by the hypothalamus. The anterior pituitary is controlled by releasing hormones that are carried in the blood from the hypothalamus. The posterior pituitary is a neural extension of the hypothalamus.

Sex hormones have two distinct kinds of effects, depending on the stage of development at which they are present. Androgens are necessary during an early critical period for the development of male genitalia and behavior in mammals. The absence of androgens results in a phenotypic female. Androgens administered to a genetic female during the critical period at least partially masculinize her genitals and behavior. In rodents androgen appears to exert its masculinizing effects on behavior by being converted, intracellularly, to estrogen. Injections of extra estrogen can masculinize females' behavior patterns. A female is not masculinized by her own estrogen because it is bound to alpha-fetoprotein. Hormones may also have organizing effects on nonsexual characteristics, such as play patterns, aggressiveness, life expectancy, and parental behavior.

Organizing effects are permanent. However, when sex hormones are administered during adulthood, they tend to elicit whatever behavior patterns were organized during development. Rodents' sexual behavior is totally dependent on the activational effects of hormones in adulthood. Estrogens enhance sensory responsiveness of the pubic area of female rats. The neurotransmitter dopamine is important for masculine sexual behavior. Female cats and dogs are dependent on estrogen for induction of attractivity and the proceptive and receptive aspects of sexual behavior.

Male cats and dogs are somewhat less dependent, especially if they have had previous sexual experience. Primates, on the other hand, are influenced by adult hormones, but sexual activity is not highly correlated with hormone levels in many species, especially humans. Testosterone increases men's sexual interest, and oxytocin may enhance sexual pleasure.

In women and certain other female primates, menstrual cycles result from interaction between the hypothalamus, pituitary, and ovaries. Follicle-stimulating hormone (FSH) from the anterior pituitary stimulates the growth of ovarian follicles and the secretion of estrogen from the follicles. Increasing estrogen at first decreases the release of FSH, but near the middle of the cycle, it somehow causes a sudden surge of luteinizing hormone (LH) and FSH. These hormones cause an ovum to be released and cause the uterine lining to proliferate. They also cause the remnant of the follicle (the corpus luteum) to release progesterone, which further prepares the uterus for implantation of a fertilized ovum. Progesterone inhibits release of LH; therefore, near the end of the cycle, all hormones are low, resulting in menstruation if fertilization does not occur. If the ovum is fertilized, estradiol and progesterone increase throughout the pregnancy. Combination birth-control pills contain estrogen, which suppresses the release of FSH early in the cycle, and progesterone, which inhibits the secretion of LH. Both estrogens and testosterone may increase women's sexual interest.

Hormones also have activational effects on nonsexual behaviors. Testosterone probably enhances aggression in many species, including humans. However, this influence probably is not a major determinant of violent behavior.

Puberty is influenced by weight and other factors. The hypothalamus begins to release bursts of luteinizing hormone releasing hormone (LHRH), which stimulates the pituitary to secrete LH and FSH, which in turn stimulate the gonads to release estradiol or testosterone.

Parental behavior in rodents can be rapidly induced by hormonal patterns characteristic of the time of delivery. This suggests that the immediate maternal behavior that occurs with delivery may be under hormonal control. However, repeated exposure to pups can induce parental behavior after 5 to 10 days, even in males and in females without ovaries. Maternal behavior consists of numerous acts, which may be elicited by specific stimuli, such as licking pups to get salt from the birth fluids and the pups' urine.

Early fetal gonadal structures may differentiate in either a male or a female direction, depending on the presence or absence of androgen. If a female is exposed to excess androgen during the critical period for sex differentiation, she may develop structures intermediate between those of a normal female and a normal male. The genital structure is too large to be a clitoris and too small to be a penis, and the labia are partially joined to produce the suggestion of a scrotum. Such an individual is called an intersex or pseudohermaphrodite. Most intersexes have been reared as females, since they are usually infertile, and it is easier to feminize the genitals surgically than to masculinize them. Most intersexes are more or less satisfied with their assigned sex, though others are not. A genetic male may develop a relatively normal female appearance and gender identity because of androgen insensitivity (testicular feminization). In the Dominican Republic some genetic males lack an enzyme that converts testosterone to DHT (5-alpha-dihydrotestosterone). Because DHT is more effective than testosterone for masculinizing the genitals, these boys appeared to be girls early in life; however, they became masculinized by high levels of testosterone at puberty. They then developed male gender identity, which was consistent with their prenatal testosterone. It was more difficult for a genetic male, whose penis was accidentally removed at birth, to develop a female identity. All of these cases suggest that prenatal hormones play an important role in determining gender identity, although environmental factors also influence this process.

Genetic factors may promote homosexual orientation in both men and women. The gene that contributes to male homosexuality appears to be on the X chromosome, and therefore is inherited from the mother. A gene that increases homosexuality, and therefore decreases reproductive success, would be expected to be selected against in the course of evolution. However, it may produce beneficial behaviors in some people without promoting homosexual orientation. Alternatively, it may perpetuated through kin selection or by increasing the reproductive ability of the women who carry the gene. Homosexuality is not well correlated with hormone levels in adulthood. However, there is some evidence that low levels of prenatal testosterone, sometimes caused by stress, may predispose males to homosexuality in adulthood. These stress effects may be mediated by endorphins and may be influenced by social experiences after birth. Some women whose mothers took diethylstilbestrol (DES) to prevent miscarriage, may have increased bisexual or homosexual responsiveness. Some brain structures show sex differences in size. For some of these structures, including the anterior commissure, the suprachiasmatic nucleus, and the interstitial nucleus 3 of the hypothalamus, homosexual men have structures more similar in size to those of women than to those of heterosexual men. We do not know whether these differences are a cause or an effect of homosexuality, or indeed, if they are relevant at all.

KEY TERMS AND CONCEPTS

Hormones and behavior
Endocrine glands

1. Mechanisms of hormone action
   Types of hormones

Protein and peptide hormones
　　Glycoproteins
　　Induction of membrane changes
　　　　Second messenger
　　　　Cyclic AMP
　Steroid hormones
　　Cytoplasmic receptors
　　Gene expression
　　Some rapid membrane effects
　　Estrogens
　　Androgens
　　Sex-limited genes
　Thyroid hormones
　Monoamines
　　Norepinephrine
　　Dopamine
　Miscellaneous other hormones
Control of hormone release
　Hypothalamus
　Posterior pituitary
　　Neural extension of hypothalamus
　　Oxytocin
　　Vasopressin or antidiuretic hormone
　Anterior pituitary
　　Hypothalamic releasing hormones
　　Adrenocorticotropic hormone (ACTH)
　　Thyroid-stimulating hormone (TSH)
　　Follicle-stimulating hormone (FSH)
　　Luteinizing hormone (LH)
　　Prolactin
　　Somatotropin (growth hormone, GH)

2.　Organizing effects of sex hormones
　Organizing effects
　　Permanent change of anatomy
　　Sensitive stage
　Activating effects
　Sex differences in the gonads and hypothalamus
　　Gonads
　　　Ovaries
　　　Testes
　　　Müllerian ducts
　　　Wolffian ducts
　　Hypothalamus
　　　Medial preoptic area
　　　　One portion larger in males

Testosterone
    Masculinization of female rats by testosterone injections
    Little or no sex hormones: female development
    Aromatization of testosterone to estradiol
    Alpha-fetoprotein
    Survival of muscles and nerves of penis
Sex differences in nonreproductive characteristics
    Body size
    Life expectancy
    Infant care
    Aggressiveness
    Rough and tumble play

3.   Activating effects of sex hormones
Activating effects on sexual behavior
    Effects on rats
        Pudendal nerve
        Ventromedial nucleus
        Preoptic area
        Dopamine
            D_1 receptors: erection
            D_2 receptors: ejaculation
    Effects on dogs and cats
        Attractivity
        Receptivity
        Proceptivity
        Estrus
    Effects on nonhuman primates
        Estrogen: increased proceptivity
        Progesterone: decreased sexual behavior and attractivity
        Testosterone: some increase in male sexual activity
    Effects on men
        Oxytocin: orgasm and sexual pleasure
        Low testosterone: impotence (sometimes)
        Cyproterone, medroxyprogesterone: block testosterone's
            effects
    Effects on women
        Menstrual cycle
        FSH
            Promotes growth of follicle
            Increases secretion of estradiol by follicle
        Estradiol
            Decreases FSH, then causes surge of LH and FSH

LH and FSH
Release ovum
Increase secretion of progesterone by corpus luteum
(remnant of follicle)
Progesterone
Prepares lining of uterus
Inhibits LH release
Menstruation: due to decreased hormone levels
If pregnancy: estrogen and progesterone increase
Birth-control pills
Combination pill
Menopause
Estrogen: proceptive behavior
Testosterone: sexual desire and enjoyment
Activating effects on aggressive behavior
Fighting in many species linked to sex hormones
Testosterone contributes to aggression in humans

4. Puberty
Menarche
Luteinizing hormone releasing hormone

5. Parental behavior
Role of hormones
Estrogen
Progesterone
Oxytocin
Prolactin
Role of experience
Complex series of acts
Licking baby rats for salt

Variations in sexual development and sexual orientation
1. Determinants of gender identity (sex role)
Intersexes or pseudohermaphrodites
Usually reared as girls
Surgery destructive of sexual sensation
Varying degrees of satisfaction with assigned sex
Testicular feminization or androgen insensitivity
Discrepancies of sexual appearance
Penis development delayed until puberty
Accidental removal of the penis

2. Possible biological bases of sexual orientation
Genetics
Different for male vs. female homosexuality

Gene on X chromosome: increased male homosexuality
  Evolutionary selection
  May promote beneficial behavior without homosexuality in
    some people
  May be perpetuated by kin selection
  May increase reproductive success of women carrying the
    gene
Effects of hormones
  Decreased testosterone during early development of males
  Stress
    Endorphins
    Social experiences
  Diethylstilbestrol (DES) in females
Brain anatomy
  Anterior commissure
  Suprachiasmatic nucleus
  Interstitial nucleus 3 of anterior hypothalamus

SHORT-ANSWER QUESTIONS

Hormones and behavior
1. *Mechanisms of hormone action*
   a. Define "hormone." How clear is the distinction between
      hormones and neurotransmitters?

   b. What are the two major classes of hormones? What are some
      additional classes of hormones?

c. By what two major mechanisms do hormones act on the nervous system?

d. What are the major differences between control mechanisms for the anterior and posterior pituitary?

e. List the hormones released from the posterior pituitary. the anterior pituitary.

f. What are releasing hormones? Where are they produced?

2. *Organizing effects of sex hormonesn*
    a. Distinguish between organizing effects and activating effects of hormones.

b. What are Müllerian ducts? What are Wolffian ducts?

c. Describe the effects of testosterone injections during the first 10 days after birth on female rats.

d. What happens if a developing mammal is exposed to neither androgens nor estrogens during early development?

e. When is the critical period for testosterone's effects on rats? on humans?

f. By what mechanism does testosterone exert its effects on the hypothalamus?

g. Describe the effects of injections of large amounts of estrogen on female rats during the critical period.

h. What is the role of alpha-fetoprotein?

i. Describe the organizing effects of testosterone on the nerves and muscles that control the penis.

j. What are some nonreproductive characteristics that may be influenced by prenatal hormones?

3. *Activating effects of sex hormones*
    a. How important are androgens for the activation of sexual behavior in male rodents? in cats and dogs? in primates, including man?

b.   Discuss the species differences in the dependence of females on hormones.

c.   What is the pudendal nerve? What are estrogen's effects on its function?

d.   What transmitter has been implicated in the stimulation of male sexual activity? What may be its role in the progression from the early stages of copulation, which require erection, to the ejaculatory stage?

e.   Distinguish among attractivity, receptivity, and proceptivity.

f.   Describe the relationship between testosterone levels and sexual activity in men.

g.   What are the effects of cyproterone and medroxyprogesterone?

h.   List the chain of hormonal processes in the menstrual cycle.

i.   What are the two effects of follicle-stimulating hormone (FSH)?

j.   Rising levels of which hormone cause a sudden surge of LH and FSH near the middle of the cycle? What are the effects of the LH and FSH?

k.   What is the corpus luteum, and what hormone does it release?

l.   What are the effects of progesterone?

m.   Describe the levels of the major hormones shortly before menstruation.

n.   How do combination birth-control pills work?

o.   What are the roles of estrogen and testosterone in women's sexual arousal?

p.   How strong is the connection between testosterone and aggression in nonhuman animals? in humans?

4. *Puberty*
   a. What is the role of weight in the age at which menarche occurs?

   b. What initiates the onset of puberty?

5. *Parental behavior*
   a. Describe the roles of hormones and experience in parental behavior of rodents.

   b. Which four hormones promote maternal behavior?

   c. Under what conditions do male rodents engage in parental behavior?

d. What are some of the components of maternal behavior in rats?

e. What is the stimulus that promotes licking of the pups by the mother? What are the effects of the licking on the young?

Variations in sexual development and sexual orientation
1. *Determinants of gender identity*
    a. What is an intersex or pseudohermaphrodite? What is the difference between a true hermaphrodite and a pseudohermaphrodite?

    b. What are some developmental influences that may produce an intersex individual?

    c. Why have most intersexes been reared as females?

d. How successful is the surgical treatment of intersexes?

e. If intersexes reject their sex assignment, what are some of the possible explanations for the rejection?

f. Describe the chromosomal pattern and the genital appearance of individuals with androgen insensitivity, or testicular feminization. What causes the unresponsiveness to androgen? What two abnormalities appear at puberty?

g. Describe two situations in which children were exposed to the prenatal hormonal pattern of one sex and then reared as the opposite sex.

h. What can we conclude from the above situations about the relative roles of prenatal hormones and upbringing in establishing gender identity?

2. *Possible biological bases of sexual orientation*
   a. Describe the evidence for a genetic predisposition towards homosexuality. Are these influences the same or different for male and female homosexuality?

   b. Is there a "gene for sexual orientation?" Why, or why not?

   c. Discuss the problems concerning evolutionary selection of any genes predisposing toward homosexuality.

   d. What are three possible explanations for the continued existence of those genes?

   e. Describe the experiments of Ingeborg Ward on the effects of stress on sex differentiation of rats. What were their results?

f. What hormone may mediate the effects of stress on sex differentiation in rats? What other factors may influence the effects of prenatal stress?

g. Summarize the evidence regarding possible prenatal stress effects on homosexual men.

h. How strong is the influence of prenatal diethylstilbestrol (DES) on homosexuality in women?

i. What are three brain structures that show a sex difference in size? In which direction is the size difference for each? How do homosexual men compare with heterosexual men and with women regarding the size of these structures?

j. Describe LeVay's evidence implicating the interstitial nucleus 3 of the hypothalamus in homosexuality.

k. If there is a consistent difference between homosexual and heterosexual men in the size of various brain nuclei, what can we conclude about the role of these nuclei in determining sexual orientation?

POSTTEST

Multiple-Choice Questions

1. Concerning hormones, which of the following is true?
    a. All hormones bind to membrane receptors and activate second messenger systems.
    b. Peptide hormones enter the cell and bind to receptors that carry them into the nucleus, where they alter gene expression.
    c. Steroid hormones enter the cell and bind to receptors that carry them into the nucleus, where they alter gene expression. They may also have rapid membrane effects.
    d. Hormones always have slow, diffuse effects, whereas neurotransmitters always have rapid, very localized effects.

2. Cyclic AMP
    a. is a glycoprotein.
    b. is a steroid hormone.
    c. is a peptide hormone.
    d. is a second messenger.

3. Androgens
    a. are present only in males; estrogens are present only in females.
    b. are present in both males and females but are produced in greater quantities in males.
    c. activate the same population of neurons as do estrogens.
    d. more than one of the above.

4. Sex-limited genes
   a. are present on the Y chromosome and therefore are lacking in females.
   b. are present on the X chromosome and therefore are unopposed and dominant in males.
   c. are present in both sexes but are activated preferentially by androgens or estrogens.
   d. are the genes that code for the production of androgens and estrogens.

5. Which of the following is true?
   a. Hormone production by the anterior pituitary is controlled by releasing hormones secreted by the hypothalamus.
   b. Hormone production by the posterior pituitary is controlled by releasing hormones from the hypothalamus.
   c. FSH is a hypothalamic releasing hormone that causes the pituitary to release LH.
   d. Estrogen is secreted by the anterior pituitary.

6. Oxytocin
   a. is also known as antidiuretic hormone.
   b. is synthesized in the hypothalamus and released from the posterior pituitary, as is vasopressin.
   c. is synthesized in and released from the anterior hypothalamus, in response to releasing hormones from the hypothalamus.
   d. controls secretions of the adrenal cortex.

7. Wolffian ducts
   a. are the precursors of the oviducts, uterus, and upper vagina.
   b. are the precursors of the male reproductive structures.
   c. are the precursors of the external genitals.
   d. all of the above.

8. If a female rat receives testosterone injections during the last few days before birth or the first few postnatal days, then in adulthood
   a. her pituitary and ovary will produce steady levels of hormones rather than cycling in the normal manner.
   b. her genitals will be completely indistinguishable from those of males.
   c. she will exhibit normal feminine sexual behavior during adulthood.
   d. all of the above.

9. A female pattern of development
   a. can be produced by giving a female mammal large amounts of estrogen during the sensitive period.
   b. can be produced in either sex in mammals by removing the gonads just after birth.
   c. can be produced in normal males by giving them estrogen in adulthood.
   d. all of the above.

10. Which of the following is true?
    a. Testosterone's organizing effects occur throughout the entire period of gestation.
    b. Estradiol masculinizes the hypothalamus by being aromatized to testosterone.
    c. Testosterone masculinizes the hypothalamus of rodents largely by being aromatized to estradiol.
    d. Alpha-fetoprotein is the enzyme that converts testosterone to estradiol.

11. High levels of testosterone during prenatal development
    a. cause female monkeys to display more rough and tumble play.
    b. may contribute to the shorter life spans of males.
    c. may contribute to the greater aggressiveness of males of most mammalian species.
    d. all of the above.

12. The activating effects of testosterone on sex behavior
    a. are mediated primarily by testosterone binding to receptors in the ventromedial hypothalamus.
    b. are limited to males.
    c. may be related to activity at dopamine synapses, including the medial preoptic area.
    d. can be observed in rodents, but not in primates, including humans.

13. Activation of female sex behavior by hormones
    a. may be mediated in part by increasing the area of skin that activates the pudendal nerve.
    b. may be enhanced by a combination of estrogen and testosterone in women.
    c. includes increases in attractivity, receptivity, and proceptivity.
    d. all of the above.

14. In nonhuman primates
    a. estrogen usually increases proceptivity more than receptivity.
    b. estrogen usually increases receptivity more than proceptivity.
    c. progesterone increases all aspects of sexual behavior in females.
    d. males are not affected by hormone levels, unlike the situation with rodents.

15. Cyproterone and medroxyprogesterone
    a. are common treatments for impotence.
    b. are occasionally used to block testosterone's effects in sex offenders.
    c. are used to increase sexual arousal in postmenopausal women.
    d. all of the above.

16. The corpus luteum
    a. is the remnant of the follicle, which releases progesterone.
    b. releases estrogen during the early part of the cycle, which causes the pituitary to release a surge of progesterone at midcycle.
    c. is the primary source of FSH.
    d. is the primary source of LH.

17. FSH
    a. is secreted from the uterus.
    b. is secreted from the follicle.
    c. stimulates the follicle to grow and produce LH.
    d. stimulates the follicle to grow, nurture the ovum, and produce estrogen.

18. Combination birth control pills
    a. contain both estrogen and progesterone.
    b. suppress the release of FSH.
    c. suppress the release of LH.
    d. all of the above.

19. What can be said of the role of testosterone in activating aggression in humans?
    a. It is the primary cause of aggression.
    b. It is irrelevant to aggression.
    c. It contributes to aggression, but is not the major determinant.
    d. It actually has a negative correlation with aggression.

20. Puberty
    a. begins when the hypothalamus begins to secrete luteinizing hormone releasing hormone in hourly bursts.
    b. is influenced by weight, among other factors.
    c. may be retarded in female rodents by the odor of other females and hastened by the odor of males.
    d. all of the above.

21. Which is true concerning rodent parental behavior?
    a. Hormones are important in eliciting parental behavior soon after giving birth for the first time.
    b. Hormones continue to be the most important factor in eliciting parental behavior throughout the entire period of care of the young.
    c. Male rats do not show any parental behavior unless they are given high doses of progesterone during prenatal development.
    d. A mother rat's dedication to her pups is so great that she overcomes her great disgust at having to swallow their urine.

22. Intersexes, or pseudohermaphrodites,
    a. usually can be made fertile with appropriate surgery.
    b. have complete sets of both male and female structures.
    c. are frequently genetic females who have been exposed to elevated levels of androgens during fetal development.
    d. are usually genetic males who have been exposed to estrogens during fetal development.

23. Intersexes reared as females
    a. are almost never happy with the sex to which they were assigned at birth.
    b. are sometimes resentful that surgical "correction" of their genitals destroys sexual sensation and makes them feel violated.
    c. provide unambiguous evidence that prenatal hormones are the primary determinant of gender identity.
    d. provide unambiguous evidence that prenatal hormones are unimportant in gender identity.

24. Androgen insensitivity (testicular feminization)
    a. is characterized by normal amounts of testosterone but a lack of receptors to carry it to the nucleus.
    b. results in an individual who appears to be completely female but fails to menstruate at puberty and has no pubic hair.
    c. cannot be alleviated by giving injections of testosterone.
    d. all of the above.

25. Certain genetic males in the Dominican Republic
    a. lack the enzyme that converts testosterone to estradiol.
    b. lack the enzyme that converts testosterone to DHT (5-alpha-dihydrotestosterone)
    c. are usually reared as boys, but adapt easily to a feminine sexual identity when they begin to produce high levels of estrogen at puberty.
    d. are usually reared as girls, but are completely unable to adapt to their new male gender identity when high levels of testosterone at puberty cause growth of a penis.

26. A genetic contribution to homosexuality
    a. may be carried by a gene on the X chromosome that promotes homosexuality in males.
    b. may be carried by a gene on the Y chromosome that promotes homosexuality in males.
    c. is probably the same for male and female homosexuals.
    d. has been disproven, since evolution strongly selects against any genes that would interfere with reproduction.

27. Male homosexuality
    a. is highly correlated with low levels of testosterone in adulthood.
    b. is highly correlated with high levels of estrogen in adulthood.
    c. may be associated with increased stress during prenatal development.
    d. may be redirected to heterosexuality by injections of testosterone in adulthood.

28. Diethylstilbestrol (DES)
    a. can be used to change the sexual orientation of homosexual men.
    b. can be used to change the sexual orientation of homosexual women.
    c. administered to mothers during pregnancy may slightly increase the likelihood of bisexuality or homosexuality in their sons.
    d. administered to mothers during pregnancy may slightly increase the likelihood of bisexuality or homosexuality in their daughters.

29. The interstitial nucleus 3 of the anterior hypothalamus
    a. is smaller in women and homosexual men than in heterosexual men.
    b. is larger in women and homosexual men than in heterosexual men.
    c. is smaller in homosexual men than in either women or heterosexual men, primarily because the AIDS virus is known to kill neurons in that site more than in the rest of the brain.
    d. is now known to be the primary brain center that determines sexual orientation.

Answers to Multiple-Choice Questions

1. c	6. b	11. d	16. a	21. a	26. a
2. d	7. b	12. c	17. d	22. c	27. c
3. b	8. a	13. d	18. d	23. b	28. d
4. c	9. b	14. a	19. c	24. d	29. a
5. a	10. c	15. b	20. d	25. b	

Diagram

Label the following structures of the endocrine system: hypothalamus, pituitary, pineal gland, adrenal gland, ovary, placenta, testis, pancreatic islets, parathyroid, thyroid, thymus.

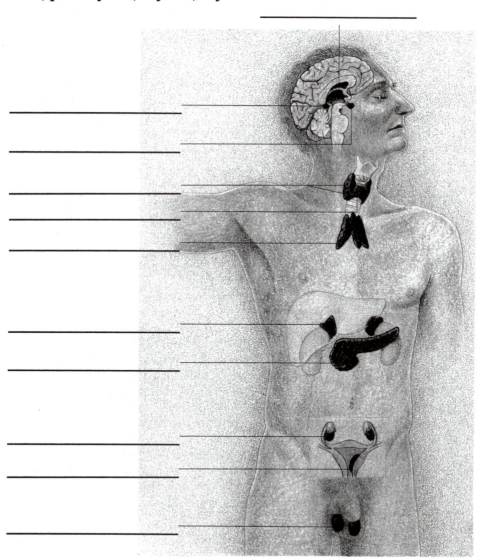

12

EMOTIONAL BEHAVIORS AND STRESS

INTRODUCTION

Activity of the autonomic nervous system, composed of the opposing sympathetic and parasympathetic divisions, has been associated with certain emotional states. For example, sympathetic activity increases when a person is nervous. The polygraph test takes advantage of this fact; recordings of heart rate, blood pressure, breathing rate, and galvanic skin response are thought to reflect a person's nervousness.

Psychosomatic illnesses are real disorders that are affected in some way by the person's personality or experiences. For example, the formation of ulcers, certain cases of sudden death, and vulnerability to certain diseases are affected by the autonomic nervous system. Predictability or apparent escapability of stressors may reduce their pathological consequences. Furthermore, chronic, uncontrollable stressors may depress the functioning of the immune system and leave an individual more vulnerable to disease. During stress, the hypothalamus directs the anterior pituitary to secrete ACTH (adrenocorticotropic hormone), which in turn stimulates the adrenal gland to secrete cortisol and other hormones. Cortisol shifts energy metabolism to increase blood sugar and decrease synthesis of proteins, including the proteins necessary for immune function. Two important elements of the immune system are the B cells, which produce antibodies that attach to and inactivate specific antigens, and the T cells, some of which attack specific "foreign" cells. Natural killer cells kill tumor cells and cells infected with viruses; their attacks are relatively nonspecific. Endorphins, released during prolonged stressful events, decrease pain and also decrease the number of natural killer cells. Stress may also accelerate the progression of AIDS. However, the relationship between experiences and illness in humans is complex and not well understood.

Researchers who have focused on the brain's role in emotion, such as Papez and MacLean, have determined that emotional feelings and behaviors are controlled and integrated largely by the hypothalamus and the limbic system. One circuit of the limbic system, including the amygdala and the hippocampus, is concerned with behaviors related to self-preservation. Another, which includes the cingulate gyrus and the septum, seems to be important for sexual pleasure. A third circuit, containing parts of the hypothalamus and anterior thalamus, may be important for cooperative social behavior.

Electrical stimulation of several areas of the limbic system can be very reinforcing. Rats frequently choose electrical stimulation in preference to food, water, avoidance of foot shock, or caring for their own pups. Humans describe stimulation of certain brain areas as pleasant, frequently with sexual overtones, but the experience does not appear to be one of ecstasy. Both catecholamine and endorphin synapses have been implicated in reward mechanisms. The medial forebrain bundle, which contains the main ascending dopamine pathway, seems to be especially important for reinforcement. Opiates may work in part by inhibiting GABA-ergic cells that in turn inhibit dopaminergic cells; in other words, they disinhibit (increase) dopamine release.

The amygdala, especially its central nucleus, seems to be a key area for anxiety. Its output to the hypothalamus controls autonomic responses, and its connections to the hindbrain elicit the skeletal responses of flinching, freezing, and other skeletal responses. Much of its input comes directly from the thalamus, rather than from the cerebral cortex, which suggests that the information is relayed rapidly but is not highly detailed. Anxiety is commonly treated with benzodiazepine tranquilizers. These drugs exert their effect at the "benzodiazepine receptor" on the $GABA_A$ receptor complex, thereby facilitating the binding of GABA to its own receptor at the complex. The binding of GABA increases the flow of chloride ions across the membrane. Barbiturates, which also have been used to treat anxiety, bind to a separate receptor on the same $GABA_A$ complex, thereby facilitating GABA binding. Beta-carbolines and endozepines, including diazepam-binding inhibitor (DBI), block the effects of diazepam and other benzodiazepines, thereby increasing anxiety. An overresponsive sympathetic nervous system is suspected of playing a role in panic attacks. Increases in carbon dioxide or lactate, which may be caused by stress or exercise, may be misinterpreted as signals of suffocation and lead to a panic attack.

Electrical stimulation of several areas of the hypothalamus and midbrain can elicit a quiet biting attack (predatory attack). Stimulation of other areas of the hypothalamus, the amygdala, and the brainstem can elicit an affective (emotional) attack. Lesions of the amygdala frequently, but not always, result in diminished aggressiveness. One characteristic of individuals with such lesions is difficulty in interpreting social stimuli, which results in failure to recognize threatening stimuli. In humans, temporal lobe epilepsy sometimes seems to be associated with unprovoked violence. Antiepileptic drugs frequently control the epilepsy and the violence; however, for extremely violent individuals who are not helped by drugs, lesions of the amygdala have sometimes reduced the violence and/or the epilepsy. Low serotonin turnover has also been implicated in aggressiveness, both in rodents and in humans. However, the mechanism linking serotonin turnover and aggressive behavior is not understood.

237

KEY TERMS AND CONCEPTS

Emotion, autonomic nervous system arousal, and health problems

1. Role of the autonomic nervous system in emotional behaviors
   Sympathetic nervous system
   Parasympathetic nervous system
   Importance of interpretation of stimuli
   Measures of autonomic arousal
   > Polygraph
   > Galvanic skin response

2. Emotions, autonomic responses, and health
   Posttraumatic stress disorder
   Behavioral medicine
   Psychosomatic illnesses
   Ulcer formation
   > Executive monkeys and rats
   > Passive monkeys and rats
   > Predictable vs. unpredictable shocks
   > Parasympathetic rebound
   Voodoo death and related phenomena
   > Curt Richter's swimming rats
   > Excessive parasympathetic activity

3. Chronic stress, the immune system, and health
   Hypothalamus--pituitary--adrenal cortex
   > Adrenocorticotropic hormone (ACTH)
   > Cortisol
   >> Increased blood sugar and metabolism
   >> Decreased protein synthesis
   Immune system
   > Leukocytes
   >> Bone marrow, thymus, spleen, lymph nodes
   >> Macrophages
   >> B cells
   >>> Antibodies
   >>> B memory cells
   >> T cells
   >>> Directly attack intruder
   >>> Helper T cells
   >> Natural killer cells
   > Antigens

Effects of stress on the immune system
    Psychoneuroimmunology
    Endorphins

Reinforcement, escape and attack behaviors, and the brain
1. The limbic system and emotions
    Hypothalamus, hippocampus, amygdala, olfactory bulb, septum, parts
        of thalamus and cerebral cortex
    Temporal lobe epilepsy
    MacLean's circuits
        Self preservation: amygdala and hippocampus
        Sexual enjoyment: cingulate gyrus and septum
        Cooperative social behavior and sexuality: Hypothalamus and
            anterior thalamus

2. Brain activity and reinforcement
    Self-stimulation of the brain
        Septal area
        Temporal lobe
        Medial forebrain bundle
        Dopamine
        Opiates and endorphin synapses

3. Fear and anxiety
    The amygdala and anxiety
        Startle response
        Central nucleus of amygdala
            Output to hypothalamus: autonomic responses
            Output to hindbrain: skeletal responses
        Input from thalamus
            Rapid, not detailed
            Some fear conditioning in thalamus
        Lateral and basolateral amygdala
            Additional fear conditioning
            Pain information
        Relevance to humans
            Phobias
            Posttraumatic stress disorder
    Anxiety-reducing drugs
        Barbiturates
        Benzodiazepines
            Diazepam (Valium)
            Chlordiazepoxide (Librium)
            Alprazolam (Xanax)

GABA$_A$ (gamma amino butyric acid) receptor complex
    Chloride channel
    Benzodiazepines
    Picrotoxin
    Barbiturates and hormone metabolites
    Alcohol
Beta-carbolines
Endozepines: endogenous antibenzodiazepines
    Diazepam-binding inhibitor (DBI)
Panic disorder
    Overresponsive sympathetic nervous system
    Exercise or stress
    Lactate
    Carbon dioxide
    Hyperventilation
    Tranquilizers and psychotherappy

4. Aggressive behaviors
Quiet biting attack (predatory attack)
    Perifornical nucleus of hypothalamus, other areas
    Attack, play, withdrawal
Affective attack
    Hypothalamus, amygdala, brainstem
        Rabies
    Interpretation of social stimuli
    Temporal lobe epilepsy
        Antiepileptic drugs
        Psychosurgery
            Surgical destruction of amygdala
Serotonin synapses and aggressive behavior
    Turnover
    5-HIAA (5-hydroxy-indole-acetic acid)
    Violent suicide
    5-HT$_2$ receptors in cerebral cortex
    Tryptophan

SHORT-ANSWER QUESTIONS

Emotion, autonomic nervous system arousal, and health problems

1. *Role of the autonomic nervous system in emotional behaviors*
   a. What are the roles of the sympathetic and parasympathetic nervous systems?

   b. What did Malcuit's study show about the way perceptions of controllability of distressful events can influence autonomic response to the event?

   c. What does the polygraph test actually measure? What is the galvanic skin response?

   d. What is the theory behind the use of the polygraph? How reliably does it indicate truthfulness? Why?

2. *Emotions, autonomic responses, and health*
   a. What are the assumptions of behavioral medicine? What
      problem have some adherents inadvertently caused?

   b. What evidence suggests that autonomic responsiveness is related
      to "personality?" To what illnesses does such overresponsiveness
      make one more vulnerable?

   c. How real are psychosomatic disorders?

   d. Describe the experimental conditions and the results of Brady et
      al.'s "executive monkey" experiment.

   e. Why was it important in Brady et al.'s experiment to have a
      passive monkey receiving the same number and pattern of shocks
      as the executive monkey? What is one criticism of the design?

f. What did Foltz and Millett find when one "passive" monkey was paired successively with three different "executives?"

g. In what way do the results of "executive rat" experiments differ from those of similar experiments with monkeys? What is one possible explanation for the difference?

h. When do shock-induced ulcers form, and what promotes them?

i. What is meant by "rebound overactivity" of the parasympathetic nervous system? How might this explain why a person may faint after escaping from something frightening?

j. How might human voodoo deaths be explained physiologically?

k. Describe Richter's experiment with swimming rats?

l. What was the cause of death in Richter's rats? Were wild or domesticated rats more likely to die? What procedure averted death of the dewhiskered rats?

3. *Chronic stress, the immune system, and health*
   a. Describe the steps in the control of cortisol secretion from the adrenal cortex.

   b. What are cortisol's major effects on blood sugar and metabolism? How does this affect the immune system?

   c. What are the most important cells of the immune system? Where are these cells produced?

d.   What are antigens? How was the name "antigen" derived?

e.   What is the role of macrophages? What are two roles of T cells?

f.   What are the roles of B memory cells and of natural killer cells?

g.   Describe the evidence suggesting that stress impairs the function of the immune system.

h.   What is another mechanism, besides increased cortisol release, by which stress affects the immune system? How large are the effects of stress, and of coping, on immune function?

i. Why may the results of experiments on stress and tumors in rats not be fully applicable to humans? What factors, other than immune system suppression, may impair the health of people under stress?

Reinforcement, escape and attack behaviors, and the brain

1. *The limbic system and emotions*
   a. List the major components of the limbic system.

   b. Describe Papez's contributions to the understanding of the neural basis of emotion.

   c. What evidence did MacLean provide in support of Papez's theory? What is Dostoyevskian epilepsy?

d.   According to MacLean, which structures within the limbic system affect behavior related to self-preservation? Which are concerned with sexual enjoyment? Which are important for social cooperation?

2.   *Brain activity and reinforcement*
    a.   How were the brain mechanisms of pleasure and reinforcement discovered?

    b.   Compare rats' reactions to electrical stimulation of reinforcing areas of the brain with their reactions to various natural reinforcements.

    c.   Describe the self-reports of reinforcing brain stimulation in humans.

d. What is one particularly reliable area for self-stimulation? What is its relationship to the transmitter dopamine?

e. Which group of transmitters, besides dopamine, contributes to reinforcement? How do opiates increase the release of dopamine?

3. *Fear and anxxiety*
    a. Why should researchers be interested in the startle response? What kind of control group is needed when using the startle response to study "fear signals?"

    b. What is a key brain area for learned fears? Which nucleus within this area seems especially important for "fear signals?"

c. What are the main output connections of the amygdala? What does each control?

d. What brain structure provides much of the input to the amygdala? Why was this discovery a surprise to researchers? What can we infer about the speed of processing and the precision of this input?

e. What two areas, in addition to the central nucleus of the amygdala, may contribute to fear conditioning?

f. What two types of drugs have been used to reduce anxiety? What are the relative advantages and disadvantages of the two types?

g.   When a benzodiazepine molecule attaches to its receptor, what happens to the GABA$_A$ synapse? What effect does this have on the flow of chloride ions across the cell membrane?

h.   How do picrotoxin, alcohol, and barbiturates affect this process?

i.   What chemicals produced by the brain affect the benzodiazepine receptors. What are their pharmacological and psychological effects? Why is the term endozepine confusing?

j.   Increases in blood levels of what two molecules can trigger panic attacks? Under what conditions do these chemicals normally increase?

k.   Explain the role of hyperventilating in panic disorder.

l. In what two ways do tranquilizers help people with panic disorder?

m. Which two transmitters are implicated in panic attacks?

4. *Aggressive behaviors*
   a. Describe the behavioral characteristics, and brain areas that organize, quiet biting attack and affective attack.

   b. What is one explanation of a cat's "play" behavior with its prey?

   c. What are the effects of stimulation of the amygdala on aggressive behavior? What are the usual effects of amygdala damage?

d. How does rabies lead to violent behavior?

e. What evidence suggests that damage to the amygdala changes how animals interpret information?

f. What are two possible explanations for the differences in effect of amygdala lesions in the three dominant monkeys in Rosvold et al.'s experiment?

g. What happens in the brain during an epileptic seizure?

h. What are the behavioral effects of temporal lobe epilepsy? Is violence an inevitable symptom?

i. What are two forms of medical or surgical treatment for frequent unprovoked violence?

j. What transmitter abnormality appears to be associated with aggressive behavior? How can it be measured?

k. Describe the experimental evidence in rats for this relationship.

l. Describe the evidence implicating low serotonin turnover in humans as a factor in aggressive behavior?

m. What is one theory about the role of serotonin in behavior?

POSTTEST

Multiple-Choice Questions

1. Which of the following statements about the parasympathetic nervous system is *not* true?
    a. It rebounds with overactivity when a stimulus that strongly excites the sympathetic nervous system is removed.
    b. It becomes activated when a person faces a stressor that is known to be uncontrollable.
    c. Its overactivity following times of stress helps to prevent ulcers.
    d. Its activity prepares the body for digestion and relaxation.

2. The polygraph
    a. measures heart and breathing rates and electrical conductance of the skin.
    b. measures epinephrine levels.
    c. is virtually 100 percent accurate in detecting lies.
    d. can discriminate extremely accurately among anger, fear, and intense happiness.

3. Psychosomatic disorders
    a. produce symptoms that are only imaginary.
    b. occur most frequently in people with very sluggish and underactive sympathetic nervous systems, because these people cannot respond effectively to stress.
    c. may occur more often in people with highly responsive sympathetic nervous systems.
    d. have recently been shown to have little or nothing to do with personality.

4. Brady et al.'s "executive monkey" experiment
    a. was flawed by the fact that only the executive monkey got shocks.
    b. was inconclusive because only the passive monkey was restrained in a chair.
    c. was inconclusive because both monkeys got ulcers about equally.
    d. was flawed by the fact that monkeys were not assigned randomly to executive and passive roles.

5. Foltz and Millet's version of the "executive monkey" experiment
   a. demonstrated that passive monkeys could get ulcers if they were repeatedly paired with untrained executives.
   b. reaffirmed Brady et al.'s findings that passive monkeys did not get ulcers.
   c. demonstrated that monkeys, but not rats, are capable of developing ulcers.
   d. was carefully controlled in that the passive monkey received only as many shocks as any one of the executive monkeys.

6. Weiss's experiments with "executive rats"
   a. demonstrated that executive rats got more ulcers than did passive rats.
   b. indicated that executive rats were less were less effective than were executive monkeys at preventing shocks; therefore, both executive and passive rats received numerous shocks, which the passive rats could neither predict nor control.
   c. suggested that shocks were not very stressful to rats because evolution has equipped them with a protective mechanism against brief bursts of electrical activity.
   d. demonstrated that monkeys got more ulcers than rats because monkeys have more responsive autonomic nervous systems.

7. Shock-induced ulcers
   a. probably form during the parasympathetic rebound after the shock-avoidance period.
   b. probably form during periods of high sympathetic nervous activity.
   c. were found in Richter's swimming rats.
   d. can sometimes be prevented by introducing brief, mild stressors during the rest period after stress.

8. Voodoo death occurs only
   a. if a witch doctor has special powers.
   b. in very primitive societies.
   c. if the victim believes in the hex or pronouncement.
   d. in people with an underresponsive parasympathetic nervous system.

9. Curt Richter found that
   a. cutting off a rat's whiskers immediately before putting it into a tank of water resulted in its struggling frantically and then sinking suddenly to the bottom, dead.
   b. laboratory rats, but not the stronger wild ones, were most susceptible to the sudden death phenomenon.
   c. rats' whiskers are critical for swimming, since removing them at any time interval before the test resulted in the animals' sudden death.
   d. all of the above are true.

10. Cortisol
    a. is secreted by the anterior pituitary gland.
    b. serves primarily to activate a sudden burst of "fight or flight" activity associated with the sympathetic nervous system.
    c. serves primarily to decrease metabolic activity in order to save energy for later stresses.
    d. shifts energy away from synthesis of proteins, including those necessary for the immune system, and towards increasing blood sugar.

11. Macrophages
    a. are specialized to produce antibodies.
    b. become B memory cells when activated by Helper T cells.
    c. engulf microorganisms and display antigen of the microorganism.
    d. are useless until they are activated by B cells.

12. Stress
    a. is by far the major factor in the success of a person's immune system in mounting an attack.
    b. causes the release of endorphins, which suppress certain immune responses.
    c. is an important activator of natural killer cells and therefore enhances immune function.
    d. all of the above.

13. Papez's circuit
    a. is a pathway exclusively devoted to the production of rage and fear.
    b. consists primarily of areas of the cerebral cortex.
    c. is the path by which epileptic activity travels from one side of the brain to the other.
    d. is now referred to as the "limbic system."

14. According to MacLean's hypothesis, which of the following pairs of structures and functions are most appropriate?
    a. amygdala and hippocampus -- self-preservation
    b. cingulate gyrus and septum -- social cooperation
    c. parts of hypothalamus and anterior thalamus -- self-preservation
    d. amygdala and hippocampus -- sexual pleasure

15. Which of the following is *not* true?
    a. Humans find self-stimulation of the brain so pleasurable that they prefer it to having sex.
    b. Dopamine activity may play a part in reinforcement.
    c. Endorphin synapses may play a role in reinforcement.
    d. Self-stimulation is frequently preferred by rats over food, water, shock avoidance, and their own pups.

16. Electrical stimulation of the brain
    a. is almost always painful.
    b. is usually reinforcing if the electrode is located in the medial forebrain bundle.
    c. elicits lever pressing primarily because it stimulates involuntary paw movements.
    d. is reinforcing, no matter which area of the brain is stimulated.

17. The brain area that seems to be especially important for learned fears is
    a. the basolateral nucleus of the thalamus.
    b. the central nucleus of the hypothalamus.
    c. the central nucleus of the amygdala.
    d. the entire hippocampus.

18. Output from the amygdala to the hypothalamus controls
    a. the intensity of sensory input to the organism.
    b. innate, rather than learned, fears.
    c. skeletal movements of the startle response.
    d. autonomic fear responses, such as increased blood pressure.

19. Much of the input to the amygdala
    a. comes from the cortex and is very detailed.
    b. comes from the thalamus and is not very detailed, but is rapidly transmitted.
    c. comes from the hypothalamus, and concerns only visual and auditory stimuli.
    d. comes directly from the peripheral sensory receptors, and is therefore very rapidly transmitted.

20. Librium, Valium, and Xanax
    a. are even more habit-forming than barbiturates.
    b. are benzodiazepines.
    c. act exclusively on catecholamine synapses.
    d. all of the above.

21. The benzodiazepines
    a. directly stimulate the same receptor sites that GABA stimulates.
    b. decrease the membrane's permeability to chloride ions.
    c. attach to receptors on the $GABA_A$ receptor complex, thereby facilitating GABA binding.
    d. block $GABA_A$ synapses.

22. Which of the following is true?
    a. Alcohol displaces benzodiazepines from their receptors, thereby disrupting GABA transmission.
    b. Alcohol produces its antianxiety effects by binding specifically to the picrotoxin site and increasing chloride flow.
    c. Picrotoxin increases the flow of chloride ions through the $GABA_A$ receptor.
    d. Endozepines, including diazepan-binding inhibitor (DBI), are actually endogenous antibenzodiazepines, which inhibit GABA transmission.

23. Which of the following is true of people who are prone to panic attacks?
    a. Their brain may misinterpret increases in blood lactate and carbon dioxide as signs of suffocation.
    b. They may have an overresponsive parasympathetic nervous system.
    c. They should hyperventilate at the first sign of panic, in order to avert a full-blown attack.
    d. They are more prone to attacks when they are in control of a situation, because they have to make decisions.

24. People with obsessive-compulsive disorder
    a. can be treated successfully with clomipramine or fluvoxamine, which inhibit the reuptake of serotonin at the synapse.
    b. have increased metabolic rates in the caudate nucleus and parts of the frontal cortex.
    c. have their symptoms aggravated by drugs that inhibit serotonin synthesis and release.
    d. all of the above.

25. Predatory attack
    a. is otherwise known as affective attack.
    b. sometimes includes "playing" with the prey, probably in defensive maneuvers.
    c. is almost completely inhibited by benzodiazepine tranquilizers.
    d. is usually elicited by feelings of intense anger.

26. Lesions of the amygdala
    a. produce difficulty in interpreting social stimuli.
    b. totally abolish aggressiveness in all animals.
    c. lead to a state that resembles manic-depressive disorder.
    d. usually decrease the frequency of quiet biting attack, but increase affective attack.

27. Temporal-lobe epilepsy
    a. is almost invariably associated with violence.
    b. is generally untreatable except by surgery.
    c. symptoms include hallucinations, lip smacking or other repetitive acts, and, in about 10% of cases, violence.
    d. can frequently be improved with antidepressant drugs.

28. Which of the following is true?
    a. Mice with low levels of serotonin turnover are abnormally placid.
    b. Drugs that facilitate the production and release of serotonin increase aggressive behavior.
    c. Serotonin turnover has been found to be lower than normal in depressed humans who commit suicide by violent means.
    d. All of the above are true.

Answers to Multiple-Choice Questions

1. c	7. a	13. d	19. b	25. b
2. a	8. c	14. a	20. b	26. a
3. c	9. a	15. a	21. c	27. c
4. d	10. d	16. b	22. d	28. c
5. a	11. c	17. c	23. a	
6. b	12. b	18. d	24. d	

13

THE BIOLOGY OF LEARNING AND MEMORY

INTRODUCTION

Learning depends upon changes within single cells, which then work together as a system to produce adaptive behavior. Different kinds of learning and memory may relie on different neural mechanisms. Classical conditioning establishes a learned association between a neutral stimulus and a stimulus that evokes a reflexive response. As a result, the previously neutral stimulus comes to evoke the reflexive response. Operant conditioning is the increase or decrease in a behavior as a result of reinforcement or punishment. In operant, but not classical, conditioning the learner controls the presentation of reinforcements and punishments. Other forms of learning, such as bird song learning, may fall outside the categories of classical or operant conditioning.

Ivan Pavlov hypothesized that all learning is based on simple neural connections formed between two brain areas active at the same time. Karl Lashley tested this hypothesis by making various cuts that disconnected brain areas from each other and by removing varying amounts of cerebral cortex after rats had learned mazes or discrimination tasks. To his surprise, he found that no particular connection or part of the cortex was critical for any task. Lashley assumed that all learning occurred in the cortex and that all types of learning relied on the same physiological mechanism. Recent evidence suggests that certain subcortical nuclei may be important for specific types of learning and that several different neural mechanisms underlie different types of learning.

Memory can be divided into several types: short-term vs. long-term, reference vs. working, explicit vs. implicit, and declarative vs. procedural. Some short-term memories are consolidated rapidly into long-term memory; others are consolidated more slowly; most are not consolidated at all. The process of consolidation can be disrupted by head trauma, and especially by damage to the hippocampus. High levels of blood glucose, released by epinephrine in the bloodstream, facilitate consolidation. Explicit memory is memory of facts or specific events; implicit memories can be detected as indirect influences on behavior, and does not require recollection of specific information. Declarative memory is memory that people can state in words, whereas procedural memory consists of motor skills. Most declarative memories are explicit, and most procedural memories are implicit; however, it may be difficult to classify memories precisely.

Richard F. Thompson has localized one type of learning, classical conditioning of the eyeblink response in rabbits, to the lateral interpositus nucleus of the cerebellum. The red nucleus, a midbrain motor center, is necessary for the motor expression of the eyeblink response, but not formation of the memory. Neurons in the cerebral cortex can also change their responsiveness to stimuli as a result of learning.

Information about memory has been obtained from studies of three major syndromes involving amnesia in humans. The main cognitive deficits in all three syndromes are inability to form new long-term declarative (explicit) memories. One syndrome results from hippocampal damage and is exemplified by the patient H. M., who had bilateral removal of the hippocampus to relieve incapacitating epilepsy. Following surgery, H. M. suffered extensive anterograde amnesia and moderate retrograde amnesia. The second disorder, Korsakoff's syndrome, occurs almost exclusively in severe alcoholics and is characterized by apathy, confusion, and both retrograde and anterograde amnesia. It is caused by prolonged thiamine deficiency, which results in loss of neurons throughout the brain, especially in the mamillary bodies of the hypothalamus and the dorsomedial thalamus, which projects to prefrontal cortex. In addition to their deficit in explicit memory, Korsakoff's patients also have difficulty recalling the temporal order of events. The third human memory disorder is Alzheimer's disease, which is characterized by progressive forgetfulness, leading to disorientation. The brains of Alzheimer's victims reveal widespread neural degeneration, especially in the cerebral cortex and hippocampus and in neurons that release acetylcholine or norepinephrine. The most heavily damaged area is the entorhinal cortex, which communicates with the hippocampus. Plaques and tangles form in areas of degeneration. Beta-amyloid, a protein found in the plaques, may be a cause of Alzheimer's disease, or it may be simply one of the symptoms. In some cases the disease may be related to a gene on chromosome 21; mutations at or near the gene for amyloid precursor protein have been found on chromosome 21 of families with early-onset Alzheimer's disease. In other families with early-onset Alzheimer's disease, a gene on chromosome 14 has been implicated. However, Alzheimer's disease depends on a variety of genetic and nongenetic influences.

Damage to the hippocampus of animals disrupts explicit (declarative) memory. Two hypotheses of hippocampal function are that it forms a map of memory storage and that it serves as a temporary store of sensory information. The prefrontal cortex in both humans and animals may play a role similar to that of the hippocampus. Prefrontal damage impairs the ability to change responses or rules governing choices. Damage to the principal sulcus, in the dorsal prefrontal cortex, impairs temporary memory on spatial tasks. Both infant amnesia and memory problems of old people are similar to cases of damage to the hippocampus and prefrontal cortex. The hippocampus is slow to mature and degenerates, along with the prefrontal cortex, in old age.

Many researchers have studied the cellular mechanisms of learning in invertebrates, which have simple, well-defined nervous systems. Studies using *Aplysia* have demonstrated changes in single synapses during habituation, sensitization, and classical conditioning. These result from changes in the number of quanta of transmitter released. Long-term potentiation (LTP), an increased response in cells of the mammalian hippocampus, depends on stimulation of two types of glutamate receptors. Stimulation of non-NMDA receptors depolarizes the neuron, thereby displacing the magnesium ions that normally block the nearby NMDA receptors. As a result, the NMDA receptors are able to respond to glutamate, allowing both sodium and calcium ions to enter the cell. The calcium, in turn, induces the expression of some otherwise inactive genes. Although stimulation of NMDA receptors is necessary for the *establishment* of LTP, activity of these receptors is not required for its *maintenance*. Near simultaneous stimulation by two or more axons increases LTP, a process called cooperativity. LTP in the cerebral cortex has a different time course, and may rely on different mechanisms. It is not clear whether LTP depends mostly on presynaptic or postsynaptic changes, or both. Nitric oxide (NO) may be released from the postsynaptic cell in some cases, and it may elicit greater release of transmitter from the presynaptic terminal. In other cases, LTP seems to depend on increased sensitivity of non-NMDA receptors on the postsynaptic neuron. A third possibility is that the postsynaptic dendrites change shape. LTP and NMDA receptors may underlie the consolidation of some, though not all, memories and may be important in the development of connections during early critical periods. On the other hand, aging may be associated with greater resting levels of intracellular calcium, so that the small increases that accompany LTP produce less effect.

Researchers have also inquired into the roles of various drugs and hormones in memory. Interruption of protein synthesis impairs learning, as does blocking acetylcholine receptors. Physostigmine, which prolongs the effects of acetylcholine, may improve memory; however, it has unwelcome side effects. Other transmitters and hormones may also affect learning. For example, dopamine and norepinephrine in prefrontal cortex may enhance learning, and vasopressin (and its metabolite AVP_{4-9}) may focus attention on certain environmental stimuli.

KEY TERMS AND CONCEPTS

Learning, memory, amnesia, and brain functioning
1. Localized or diffuse representations of memory
    Classical conditioning
        Ivan Pavlov
        Conditioned stimulus (CS)
        Unconditioned stimulus (US)

Unconditioned response (UR)
Conditioned response (CR)
Operant conditioning
Reinforcement
Punishment
Bird-song learning
Karl Lashley
Engram
Amount of damage, not location

2. Various types of memory
Short-term memory versus long-term memory
Double dissociation of function
Consolidation of long-term memories
Reverberating circuit
Epinephrine
Glucose
Explicit memory versus implicit memory
Priming
Declarative memory versus procedural memory

3. Brain damage and impairments of implicit memory
Classical conditioning of eyelid responses in rabbits
Richard F. Thompson
Lateral interpositus nucleus of the cerebellum
Red nucleus
Midbrain motor area

4. Brain damage and impairments of explicit memory
Amnesia
H. M., a man with hippocampal damage
Severe anterograde amnesia
Moderate retrograde amnesia
Korsakoff's syndrome and other frontal-lobe damage
Thiamine deficiency
Dorsomedial thalamus
Prefrontal cortex
Both anterograde and retrograde amnesia
Loss of explicit, but not implicit, memory
Recall of temporal order of events
Alzheimer's disease
Memory loss, confusion, depression, restlessness, hallucinations, delusions, disturbances of eating, sleeping, and daily activities
Learn skills better than facts

Atrophy of cerebral cortex and hippocampus
Entorhinal cortex
Loss of acetylcholine neurons
Plaques and tangles
Beta-amyloid
Genetic and nongenetic causes
Relationship to Down's syndrome
Mutations on chromosome 21
Amyloid precursor protein
Chromosome 14

5. Role of the hippocampus, amygdala, and frontal cortex
Damage to the hippocampus in rats
Radial maze
Spatial learning
Configural conditioning
Impaired explicit memory
Damage to the hippocampus in primates
Delayed matching-to-sample test
Delayed nonmatching-to-sample test
Two hypotheses of hippocampal function
Map of memory storage
Temporary store of sensory information
Contributions of the prefrontal cortex
Damage to ventral area: perseveration
Wisconsin card-sorting task
Damage to principal sulcus: spatial problems
Delayed response task

6. Brain and memory in young and old
Infant amnesia
Greater impairment of explicit than implicit memories
Hippocampus slow to mature
Old people with memory problems
Greater impairment of explicit than implicit memories
Hippocampal degeneration
Prefrontal cortex degeneration

Mechanisms of storing information in the nervous system
1. Learning and the Hebbian synapse
Simultaneous pre- and postsynaptic activity

2. Single-cell mechanisms of invertebrate behavior change
Aplysia as an experimental animal
Plasticity

Habituation in *aplysia*
    Decreased number of quanta from sensory neuron
Sensitization in *aplysia*
    Increased number of quanta from sensory neuron
    Facilitating interneuron
    Serotonin (5-HT)
    Cyclic AMP
    Blocking of potassium channels
    Prolonged action potential
    Protein synthesis
    Long-term sensitization

3. Long-term potentiation in the mammalian brain (LTP)
    Brief but rapid series of stimuli
    Increased responsiveness for minutes, days, or weeks
    Hippocampal slice
        NMDA receptors
        Non-NMDA receptors
        Magnesium blockade of NMDA receptors
        Removal of magnesium by depolarization
        Calcium influx into postsynaptic neuron
        NMDA receptors: establish, not maintain, LTP
        Activation of gene expression
        Cooperativity
    Long-term potentiation and behavior
        Memory of frightening experience
        Modification of synapses during developmental critical period
        "Leaky" calcium channels in old age
            Higher resting calcium levels
            Less impact of LTP

4. The biochemistry of learning and memory
    Influence of protein synthesis on learning and memory
    Acetylcholine synapses and memory
        Scopolamine (blocks acetylcholine receptors)
        Physostigmine (inhibits breakdown of acetylcholine and
            prolongs its effects)
        Choline and lecithin (dietary precursors): no benefits in elderly
    Other synapses and memory
        Norepinephrine and dopamine in prefrontal cortex
    Chemical modulators of attention
        ACTH
        Vasopressin
            AVP_{4-9}

SHORT-ANSWER QUESTIONS

Learning, memory, amnesia, and brain functioning
1. *Localized or diffuse representations of memory*
   a. Describe the relationships among the conditioned and unconditioned stimuli and the unconditioned and conditioned responses in classical conditioning.

   b. Who discovered classical conditioning? What were the conditioned and unconditioned stimuli in his experiments? What was the unconditioned, and eventually the conditioned, response?

   c. What is the fundamental distinction between classical and operant conditioning? Define reinforcement and punishment in terms of operant conditioning.

   d. Why is bird-song learning difficult to classify?

e. What is an engram? What did Lashley discover in his search for the engram?

f. What two assumptions did Lashley make, which investigators have later rejected?

2. *Various types of memory*
   a. Define short-term memory and long-term memory.

   b. How did Donald Hebb explain consolidation?

   c. How do exciting experiences and epinephrine enhance memory?

d. Distinguish between explicit memory and implicit memory.

e. What is priming? Is it used to test explicit or implicit memory?

f. Distinguish between declarative memory and procedural memory.

g. What is the relationship between explicit and declarative memory? between implicit and procedural memory?

3. *Brain damage and impairments of implicit memory*
   a. What brain area was found by Richard F. Thompson to be important for classical conditioning of the eyeblink response in rabbits?

b. What area was important for the expression of the motor response, but not for the initial conditioning?

c. Describe the experiment showing conditioning of implicit memory in the auditory portions of the thalamus and cerebral cortex.

4. *Brain damage and impairments of explicit memory*
   a. Why was H. M.'s hippocampus removed bilaterally? How successful was this treatment at relieving epilepsy? What were the other effects of the surgery?

   b. What is the difference between retrograde and anterograde amnesia? Which was more severely impaired in H. M.?

c. What is the immediate cause of Korsakoff's syndrome? What are its symptoms? In what group of people does it usually occur?

d. Which brain areas show neuronal loss in Korsakoff's syndrome?

e. Describe the symptoms of Korsakoff's syndrome in terms of anterograde vs. retrograde amnesia, and explicit vs. implicit memory.

f. How are implicit and explicit memory tested?

g. What other symptom do Korsakoff's patients have, in common with patients with frontal-lobe damage?

h. Describe the symptoms of Alzheimer's disease.

i. Which brain areas are atrophied in Alzheimer's disease? Neurons containing which transmitter degenerate? What physical signs are present in areas of atrophy?

j. Why do some researchers believe that beta-amyloid may be a cause of Alzheimer's disease? What problems have been raised concerning this hypothesis?

k. Why are some cases of Alzheimer's disease thought to be related to a gene on chromosome 21? How does the chromosomal abnormality differ from that in Down's syndrome?

l. What is amyloid precursor protein? On which chromosome is the gene that determines the structure of this protein?

5. *Role of the hippocampus, amygdala, and frontal cortex*
   a.   What two kinds of errors can rats make in the radial maze.
        Which type of error do rats make after damage to the
        hippocampus?

   b.   What two hypotheses concerning hippocampal function were
        proposed, but fail to fit all the data?

   c.   What seems to be the hypothesis most consistent with the data
        concerning hippocampal function?

   d.   Describe the delayed matching-to-sample and delayed
        nonmatching-to-sample tests. Which can monkeys perform
        most easily?

   e.   What is the effect of hippocampal lesions on this type of test? of
        prefrontal cortex lesions?

272

f. Why can we conclude that memories are not stored in the
    hippocampus itself?

g. Describe two hypotheses about the role of the hippocampus in
    memory.

h. What is the anatomical relationship between the hippocampus
    and amygdala, and the prefrontal cortex?

i. Describe the effects of damage to a ventral area of the
    prefrontal cortex on the Wisconsin card-sorting task.

j. Describe the delayed response task.

k. What are the effects of damage to the principal sulcus of the prefrontal cortex on performance on the delayed response task?

6. *Brain and memory in young and old*
    a. What is infant amnesia? Is there greater retention of explicit or implicit memories?

    b. Give one physiological explanation for infant amnesia.

    c. Deterioration of which two brain areas may impair memory in old age?

    d. Which two transmitters have been found to decrease in prefrontal cortex with aging?

Mechanisms of storing information in the nervous system

1. *Learning and the Hebbian synapse*
   a. Define "Hebbian synapse." How is it related to classical conditioning?

2. *Single-cell mechanisms of invertebrate behavior change*
   a. Why should anyone be interested in the cellular mechanisms of sensitization or habituation in the lowly *Aplysia*?

   b. What possible mechanisms of habituation were ruled out experimentally? What mechanism does seem to account for habituation in *Aplysia*?

   c. How is sensitization produced experimentally in *Aplysia*? Where is the facilitating interneuron located?

d. Describe the cellular events that explain sensitization in *Aplysia.*

e. How does long-term sensitization differ from the short-term variety?

3. *Long-term potentiation in the mammalian brain*
    a. How is long-term potentiation (LTP) produced? How long does it last? In what brain area was it first discovered?

    b. Which transmitter stimulates both NMDA and non-NMDA receptors? Why non-NMDA receptors be stimulated, in addition to NMDA receptors, in order to produce LTP?

    c. What is the effect of stimulating NMDA receptors?

d.   Are NMDA receptors important for the establishment or maintenance of LTP?

e.   What is meant by "cooperativity?"

f.   Compare the temporal course of LTP in hippocampus with that in the cerebral cortex.

g.   List the three possible mechanisms of LTP.

h.   What may be the role of nitric oxide (NO) in LTP?

i. Describe an experiment showing the relevance of NMDA receptors for establishing a memory.

j. What may be the role of NMDA receptors during the critical period in early development?

k. How may "leaky" calcium channels impair memory in aged mammals?

4. *The biochemistry of learning and memory*
   a. Why is protein synthesis important for learning?

   b. What transmitter, besides glutamate, seems to be important for memory? What does scopolamine do? What are its effects on young adult humans?

c. What are the effects of physostigmine on acetylcholine synapses? How useful is this drug likely to be for people with poor memories?

d. How effective is dietary supplementation with choline and lecithin in reversing memory deficits?

e. Which other transmitters in prefrontal cortex may be important for memory? What are the synaptic effects of clonidine? What are its effects on memory after damage to catecholamine input to prefrontal cortex?

f. What are the roles of ACTH and vasopressin in learning tasks? Which metabolite of vasopressin is more effective than vasopressin itself? Are the effects of these hormones always beneficial?

g. What are two human disorders relating to the ability to focus or shift one's attention?

POSTTEST

Multiple-Choice Questions

1. In classical conditioning
   a. the meat used by Pavlov was the conditioned stimulus.
   b. the learner's behavior controls the presentation of reinforcements and punishments.
   c. a stimulus comes to elicit a response similar to the response elicited by another stimulus.
   d. bird-song learning can be fully explained in terms of CS and US.

2. Ivan Pavlov believed that learning occurs when
   a. the connection between the CS center and the US center is strengthened.
   b. the connection between the CS center and the CR center is strengthened.
   c. the CS center takes over the US center's ability to elicit a UR.
   d. cells in the US center degenerate and cells in the CS center branch diffusely.

3. Lashley successfully demonstrated that
   a. the lateral interpositus nucleus is the site of all engrams.
   b. all learning takes place in the cerebral cortex.
   c. the same neural mechanisms underlie all types of learning.
   d. none of the above.

4. Hebb's distinction between short-term and long-term memory
   a. is supported by data showing that damage to the hippocampus can disrupt formation of new long-term, but not short-term, memories.
   b. is supported by data showing that sudden head trauma disrupts memories that were formed long ago, but not memories formed just before the trauma.
   c. has been rejected by researchers because there is no double dissociation of function of the two types of memory.
   d. has recently been attributed to Pavlov, instead of Hebb.

280

5. Experiments on consolidation have shown that
   a. the most important factor promoting consolidation is the amount of time allowed for reverberating circuits to operate.
   b. an exciting experience arouses the sympathetic nervous system, which releases epinephrine, which in turn facilitates consolidation.
   c. sudden head trauma actually facilitates consolidation.
   d. all of the above are true.

6. Epinephrine in the blood facilitates memory consolidation by
   a. causing circuits to reverberate.
   b. crossing the blood-brain barrier and activating synapses in the hippocampus.
   c. raising the level of glucose in the blood.
   d. being converted into norepinephrine and then crossing the blood-brain barrier to activate synapses.

7. Your memory of what you had for dinner last night is an example of
   a. explicit memory.
   b. implicit memory.
   c. procedural memory.
   d. short-term memory.

8. Priming is useful for
   a. producing memory consolidation.
   b. testing short-term memory.
   c. testing explicit memory.
   d. testing implicit memory.

9. The lateral interpositus nucleus of the cerebellum
   a. is important for the motor expression of eyelid conditioning in rabbits, but not the actual conditioning.
   b. is important for the actual conditioning of the eyelid response.
   c. is more important for explicit than implicit memory formation.
   d. is an area that shows a great deal of damage in Korsakoff's syndrome.

10. H. M.
    a. had his hippocampus removed because of his uncontrollable violence.
    b. acquired severe epilepsy as a result of the surgery.
    c. has a terrific memory for numbers but can learn no new skills.
    d. has more severe problems learning facts than learning skills.

11. Which of the following statements applies to H. M.?
    a. He has more severe anterograde than retrograde amnesia.
    b. He is unable to learn any new skills, but can learn new facts.
    c. His deficits show conclusively that the hippocampus is the storage site for all factual memories.
    d. All of the above are true.

12. Korsakoff's syndrome
    a. occurs because alcohol dissolves proteins in the brain, thereby shrinking presynaptic endings.
    b. results from damage primarily to the hippocampus.
    c. is caused by prolonged thiamine deficiency.
    d. all of the above.

13. Patients with Korsakoff's syndrome
    a. have damage in the mamillary bodies of the hypothalamus and the dorsomedial nucleus of the thalamus, which projects to prefrontal cortex.
    b. have symptoms somewhat similar to those of patients with damage to the prefrontal cortex.
    c. have considerable loss of explicit memory, but little loss of implicit memory.
    d. all of the above.

14. Alzheimer's disease
    a. results from three copies of chromosome 21.
    b. results from a long history of excessive alcohol consumption.
    c. is characterized by widespread atrophy of the cerebral cortex (especially the entorhinal cortex), hippocampus, and neurons that release acetylcholine.
    d. is characterized by severe atrophy of the prefrontal cortex and amygdala and of neurons that release enkephalins, but relative sparing of the rest of the brain.

15. Patients with Alzheimer's disease
    a. have a nearly 100% probability of passing the disease on to their offspring.
    b. unlike H. M. and Korsakoff's patients, have more problems with implicit than explicit memory.
    c. have plaques and tangles in damaged areas of their brains.
    d. all of the above.

16. Which of the following is true of amyloid precursor protein?
    a. Fragments of it can become beta-amyloid, which is found in plaques.
    b. The gene that determines its structure is on chromosome 21.
    c. Mutations in or near the gene that determines its structure have been found in some families with early-onset Alzheimer's disease.
    d. All of the above are true.

17. Damage to the hippocampus results in
    a. rats going down a never-correct arm of the radial maze.
    b. rats going down one correct arm repeatedly.
    c. rats failing to learn to approach one visual pattern and not another.
    d. rats failing to leave the center of the radial maze.

18. Which of the following is true of the hippocampus?
    a. The delayed nonmatching-to-sample test can indicate hippocampal damage when the monkey has to choose between different objects every time.
    b. It may serve as a map of where memories are stored in the cortex.
    c. Its neurons may serve as a temporary store of sensory information through their continuous activity.
    d. All of the above are true.

19. Which of the following is true?
    a. Damage to a ventral portion of prefrontal cortex results in errors of perseveration.
    b. Humans with prefrontal damage have difficulty sorting cards according to any rule.
    c. The prefrontal cortex performs functions that are basically opposite those of the hippocampus.
    d. The hippocampus is the storage site of all memories.

20. Infant amnesia
    a. shows a greater loss of implicit than explicit memories.
    b. may result from low levels of blood glucose.
    c. may result from the slow development of the hippocampus.
    d. is characterized by symptoms that are essentially the opposite of those seen in old age.

21. Habituation in *Aplysia* is the result of
    a. a decrease in the number of quanta of neurotransmitter released.
    b. a decrease in the size of each quantum.
    c. decreased sensitivity of the postsynaptic cell.
    d. muscle fatigue.

22. The mechanism mediating sensitization includes
    a. the release of serotonin onto the facilitating interneuron by the sensory neuron.
    b. decreased outflow of potassium in the sensory neuron, resulting in prolonged transmitter release.
    c. the release of cyclic AMP by the sensory neuron onto the interneuron, which then alters gene expression in the interneuron.
    d. hypersensitivity of the postsynaptic cell to cyclic AMP.

23. Long-term potentiation (LTP)
    a. was first discovered in *Aplysia*.
    b. results from increased inflow of magnesium through non-NMDA receptors.
    c. requires depolarization via NMDA receptors in order to allow calcium outflow through non-NMDA receptors.
    d. requires depolarization via non-NMDA receptors in order to dislodge magnesium ions from NMDA receptors.

24. LTP
    a. is very powerful but lasts only a few seconds.
    b. may result from decreased sensitivity of the postsynaptic cell to the inhibitory transmitter glutamate.
    c. may involve nitric oxide (NO) being released from the postsynaptic cell and causing the presynaptic terminal to release more transmitter.
    d. uses the same mechanism in hippocampus and cerebral cortex.

25. Which of the following is true?
    a. Modification of synapses during the critical period in early development may depend on NMDA receptors.
    b. Scopolamine shows considerable promise as a treatment for memory disorders.
    c. Cooperativity refers to the strengthening of all synapses throughout an area of the brain by the activity on only one or two of them.
    d. A problem in aged mammals is the near total closing down of calcium channels, so that NMDA receptors can no longer let calcium flow in.

26. Vasopressin
    a.   is metabolized by the brain to form AVP_{4-9}, which focuses attention on the dominant cues in the environment.
    b.   should be especially beneficial to autistic children.
    c.   helps animals shift their attention from one stimulus to another.
    d.   all of the above.

Answers to Multiple-Choice Questions

1. c	6. c	11. a	16. d	21. a	26. a
2. a	7. a	12. c	17. b	22. b	
3. d	8. d	13. d	18. d	23. d	
4. a	9. b	14. c	19. a	24. c	
5. b	10. d	15. c	20. c	25. a	

14

LATERALIZATION AND LANGUAGE

INTRODUCTION

Each hemisphere of the brain receives sensory input primarily from the opposite side of the body and controls motor output to that side as well. The hemispheres are connected by a large bundle of fibers, the corpus callosum, as well as several smaller bundles. In humans, the eyes are connected with the brain in such a way that the left half of each retina supplies input to the left hemisphere, and vice versa. Furthermore, the left half of each retina receives input from the right half of the visual field. Therefore, the right half of the visual field projects to the left hemisphere, and vice versa. This relationship has allowed researchers to test the roles of the two hemispheres in people whose corpus callosum had been severed (to relieve epilepsy). Such studies have shown that the left hemisphere is specialized for language or "sequential, analytic" functions, whereas the right hemisphere is particularly adept at emotional expression, emotional perception, complex spatial problems, and "synthetic, holistic" tasks. Split-brain people sometimes seem to have two "selves" occupying the same body. Each half of the brain processes information and solves problems more or less independently of the other. Even in intact people, evidence for hemispheric specialization can be seen.

The corpus callosum matures gradually, and experience determines the survival of the axons that make the most functional connections across the corpus callosum. People born without a corpus callosum are different from those who had split-brain surgery in adulthood. They can verbally describe sensory input from either hand and from either visual field. They may rely on greater development of the anterior commissure and hippocampal commissure to convey information from one hemisphere to the other.

One possible basis for the lateralization of language functions in the left hemisphere is that in 65 percent of people a portion of the left temporal lobe, the planum temporale, is larger on the left side than on the right. The size difference is apparent even shortly after birth. One factor promoting left-handedness may be the male hormone testosterone, which may delay the maturation of the left hemisphere and also of the immune system. Thus, hormonal factors may at least partially account for the correlation of left-handedness, being male, dyslexia, excellence in mathematics, and immune system disorders.

Language may have evolved as a by-product of increasing intelligence; on the other hand, the increasing intelligence and the brain reorganization on which it depended, may have occurred *because* of the growing importance of language. Because new features evolve from older ones that may have served similar functions, researchers have studied the language abilities of our nearest relatives, the chimpanzees. A number of chimpanzees have been taught to communicate with their trainers, a computer, or each other using various nonspoken language systems. These animals acquire impressive vocabularies, and some have demonstrated some degree of grammatical ability. However, even after years of training, their linguistic abilities fall far short of those of young children. Pan paniscus, sometimes called pygmy chimpanzees, have shown the most impressive linguistic abilities among our primate relatives. They have learned by imitation, have used words to describe objects (as opposed to making a request) or to refer to a past event, and have created original sentences. In addition, some have learned to understand spoken English sentences. Dolphins and parrots also show some language abilities. Studies of nonhuman language abilities may provide insights about how best to teach language to brain-damaged or autistic people; they may also stimulate consideration of the unique versus shared abilities of humans and of the nature of language.

Paul Broca discovered that damage to an area of the left frontal lobe results in difficulties with pronunciation and with the use of grammatical connectives and other *closed class* grammatical forms. However, people with such damage can usually understand both written and spoken language much better than they can produce it. Carl Wernicke, on the other hand, described a pattern of deficits almost the opposite of the pattern Broca discovered: poor language comprehension, anomia (difficulty finding the right word), but fluent (though mostly meaningless) speech. This syndrome results from destruction of an area in the left temporal lobe near the primary auditory cortex. PET scans in intact adults have shown that silent reading activates only the occipital cortex, analyzing rhymes activates primarily the temporal lobe, and either reading or listening to words and stating their use activates the frontal lobe, including Broca's area.

Alexia, or word blindness, results when the left visual cortex and the posterior part of the corpus callosum (the splenium) have been damaged. Reading is impaired because information can no longer be transfered from the intact right visual cortex to language areas in the left side of the brain. Other disconnection syndromes have also been described. Genetic conditions can impair language development without noticeably affecting other functions. On the other hand, people with Williams syndrome have excellent language abilities, but are impaired in nonlalnguage skills; this syndrome appears to result from an unusual pattern of brain connections, rather than loss or absence of any specific area. Dyslexia, a reading disorder in otherwise normal people, may result from anomalies in brain lateralization. Some dyslexics' reading ability may be improved by focusing on one word at a time.

KEY TERMS AND CONCEPTS

Lateralization of function and the corpus callosum
1. Connections of the eyes to the brain's left and right hemispheres
    Right visual field-->left hemisphere (and vice versa)
        Optic chiasm
    Both ears-->both hemispheres
        Opposite side stronger

2. Effects of cutting the corpus callosum
    Epilepsy
    Split-brain humans: two minds or one?
    Left hemisphere: speech
    Right hemisphere: spatial and emotional functions
        Can understand simple speech or writing
    Hemispheric specialization in intact people
    Hemispheric differences and cognitive style: A doubtful assumption

3. Development of lateralization and its relationship to handedness
    Anatomical differences between the hemispheres
        Planum temporale
        Sylvian or lateral fissure
    Maturation of corpus callosum
        Survival of functional connections
    Development without a corpus callosum
        Anterior commissure
        Hippocampal commissure
    Handedness and language dominance
        99% of right-handed: left hemisphere for speech
        60 to 70% of left-handed: left hemisphere for speech
        High testosterone during development
            Left-handedness, dyslexia, stuttering
            Immune disorders, allergies, migraines
            Excellence in math and spatial skills

The Biological basis of language
1. The evolution of language capacities
    Relationship of intelligence to language
    Language ability of chimpanzees
        Inability to speak
        Ability to use visual symbols for words
        Use of some grammatical rules
        Difference from children
            Few original sentences
            Symbols used to request, not describe
            Difficulties with changes in word order

288

Pan paniscus (pygmy chimpanzees)
    Name without request
    Refer to past
    Creative requests
Dolphins, parrots

2. Effects of brain damage on human language
Broca's aphasia
    Nonfluent aphasia
    Difficulty in language production
        Articulation, writing, and gestures
        Omission of *closed class* of grammatical forms (prepositions, conjunctions, pronouns, helper verbs, quantifiers, tense and number endings)
        Ability to speak *open class* forms (nouns and verbs)
    Problems comprehending grammatical words and devices
Wernicke's aphasia
    Fluent aphasia
    Articulate speech
    Anomia (difficulty finding the right word)
    Poor language comprehension
PET scan studies of language processing
Other language deficits
    Word blindness (alexia) despite ability to write
        Destruction of left visual cortex
        Destruction of splenium of corpus callosum
    Inability to follow instructions to move a limb in isolation
        Disconnection of language areas from pyramidal system
        Intact primary motor cortex and pyramidal system
        Intact connections from language areas to extrapyramidal system
    Developmental language impairment
        Genetic condition impairing language development
            Difficulties with both articulation and grammar
        Williams syndrome
            Superior language skills
            Retarded in nonlanguage skills
        Dyslexia
            Anomalous lateralization of function
            Relatively unresponsive magnocellular system
            Lateral masking
            Reading one word at a time

SHORT-ANSWER QUESTIONS

Lateralization of function and the corpus callosum

1. *Connections of the eyes to the brain's left and right hemispheres*
   a. To which hemisphere(s) does the right visual field project? To which hemisphere(s) does the right half of both retinas project? To which hemisphere(s) does the right eye project?

   b. To which hemisphere(s) does the right ear project?

2. *Effects of cutting the corpus callosum*
   a. What is the corpus callosum? Why is it sometimes severed in cases of severe epilepsy? What are the effects of such an operation on overall intelligence, motivation, emotion, language, and gross motor coordination?

   b. What have we learned from split-brain humans concerning specialization of the two hemispheres? Which tasks are best accomplished by the left hemisphere?

c. Which tasks are best performed by the right hemisphere?

d. How can the two hemispheres communicate with each other in some experimental situations that were designed to study the function of only one?

e. What kinds of tasks can show hemispheric specialization in intact people? How consistent are the results?

f. How valid is the assumption that a given individual relies consistently on one hemisphere or the other, regardless of the task?

3. *Development of lateralization and its relationship to handedness*
   a. What is the planum temporale and what is its significance for language?

b.   Compare the degree of lateralization in humans, chimpanzees, and monkeys.

c.   Discuss the role of experience in the survival of neurons whose axons cross in the corpus callosum.

d.   Compare the ability of 3-year-olds and of 5-year-olds to discriminate fabrics with either one hand or different hands. What can we infer from this about the development of the corpus callosum?

e.   In what ways are people who never had a corpus callosum different from split-brain people? How are they similar?

f.   Which other major axonal connections between the two hemispheres may compensate for the lack of a corpus callosum in people born without one.

g. What percentage of right-handed people have left-hemisphere dominance for language? What percentage of left-handed people have left-hemisphere dominance for language?

h. Is the corpus callosum thicker in right- or left-handed people? What is the functional correlate of this increased thickness?

i. List the traits that have been proposed by Geschwind and Galaburda to be related to high levels of, or sensitivity to, testosterone during development.

j. What effect may testosterone have on the left hemisphere? How could this affect the development of language in boys? What may testosterone do to the immune system?

The biological basis of language
1. *The evolution of language capacities*
   a. Briefly discuss the proposal that our intelligence may have developed as a by-product of the selection for language.

   b. What are some differences between the abilities of chimps and of children to use language?

   c. What was unusual about the ability of some Pan paniscus to learn language? How does their understanding of language compare with their production of language?

   d. In what three ways do Pan paniscus differ from common chimps in language production?

   e. What are two explanations for why Pan paniscus have been more successful than other chimps at learning language?

f.　What evidence is there that nonprimate species can learn language?

2.　*Effects of brain damage on human language*
　　a.　Where is Broca's area located?

　　b.　Describe the effects of damage to Broca's area. What are closed class words?

　　c.　Locate Wernicke's area.

　　d.　Contrast the effects of damage to Wernicke's area with those of damage to Broca's area.

e. What information about language processing has been gained from PET scans?

f. What are the symptoms of damage to the left visual cortex and posterior corpus callosum? Explain this pattern of symptoms.

g. What brain damage may result in inability to follow instructions to move a limb in isolation?

h. Compare the genetic condition resulting in severe language deficits, despite otherwise normal intelligence, with the pattern of abilities seen in Williams syndrome.

i. What are some possible biological causes of dyslexia?

j. What is lateral masking? How does the pattern of lateral masking in dyslexics differ from that in normal readers?

k. What is one method of improving the ability of dyslexics to read?

POSTTEST

Multiple-Choice Questions

1. Severing the corpus callosum
    a. usually produces ulcers.
    b. usually relieves the symptoms of epilepsy.
    c. has provided evidence that linguistic abilities reside largely in the right hemisphere.
    d. none of the above.

2. A person with a bisected brain
    a. can draw pictures with a better spatial representation with the left hand than with the right.
    b. has no verbal comprehension at all in the right hemisphere.
    c. is very clumsy.
    d. more than one of the above.

3. The only way to present visual input to only the right hemisphere of a split-brain person is to
    a. flash it briefly to the left eye while the right eye is closed.
    b. flash it briefly to the right eye while the left eye is closed.
    c. flash it briefly in the left visual field while the person is looking straight ahead.
    d. flash it briefly in the right visual field while the person is looking straight ahead.

4. If the right hand of a split-brain person holds a spoon behind a screen, the person
   a. will be able to point to the spoon but will not be able to name it.
   b. will not be able either to point to it or to name it.
   c. will be able both to point to it and to name it.
   d. will be able to name it but not point to it.

5. A split-brain person sees this picture flashed briefly on a screen while he is looking at a point in the middle of the screen. The person reports seeing
   a. a woman.
   b. a bearded man.
   c. a meaningless hodge podge of lines, since the spatial perception center has been damaged.
   d. one badly constructed face of two different people.

6. People with right-hemisphere damage
   a. have trouble producing and understanding emotional facial expressions.
   b. have trouble speaking with emotional expression and understanding others' vocal emotional expression.
   c. have trouble with some complex visual and spatial tasks.
   d. all of the above.

7. Hemispheric specialization in intact people
   a. has not been demonstrated.
   b. is consistent with that observed in split-brain people but is even more dramatic.
   c. can be shown but is small and inconsistent.
   d. is the reverse of specialization in split-brain people.

8. The planum temporale
   a. includes important language areas.
   b. is larger in the right than in the left hemisphere for everyone.
   c. is equal in size in the two hemispheres at birth, indicating that maturation of language causes the size difference in adults.
   d. all of the above

9. What did Galin et al. discover when they asked 3-year-old and 5-year-old children to discriminate two fabrics?
   a. The 3-year-olds were better than the 5-year-olds.
   b. All children made fewer errors with their right hands than with their left.
   c. All children made 90 percent more errors using different hands than when using the same hand.
   d. Three-year-olds made 90 percent more errors using different hands than using the same hand, but 5-year-olds did equally well with one hand or two.

10. People who never had a corpus callosum
    a. are just like split-brain patients.
    b. can read words in either visual field and name objects that they touch with either hand.
    c. are especially fast at tasks requiring coordination of both hands.
    d. all of the above.

11. Which of the following was *not* proposed by Geschwind and Galaburda to be associated with increased testosterone during development?
    a. left-handedness
    b. deficits in mathematics
    c. dyslexia
    d. immune system disorders

12. One possible mechanism to explain the results in #11 is that
    a. testosterone may decrease the size of the corpus callosum.
    b. migraines in children may keep them from learning to read.
    c. testosterone may inhibit maturation of the right hemisphere.
    d. testosterone may inhibit maturation of the left hemisphere.

13. Pan paniscus
    a. can understand spoken English sentences.
    b. use symbols only to request objects.
    c. are unable to put symbols together in new ways to express new meanings.
    d. have learned to speak English fluently.

14. A patient has great difficulty in articulating words and a tendency to omit endings and abstract words, but little difficulty comprehending spoken and written words. The patient probably has damage in
    a. Broca's area.
    b. Wernicke's area.
    c. the corpus callosum.
    d. primary motor cortex controlling muscles of articulation.

15. A second patient has difficulty naming objects and understanding both spoken and written language; speech is fluent but not very meaningful. You suspect that the patient has damage in
    a. Broca's area.
    b. Wernicke's area.
    c. the anterior commissure and hippocampal commisure.
    d. left visual cortex and posterior corpus callosum.

16. PET scans of intact humans showed that
    a. analyzing rhymes activated only occipital cortex.
    b. reading silently activated all areas that process language.
    c. reading silently activated only occipital cortex.
    d. frontal cortex processed only spoken, not written, language.

17. Word blindness despite ability to write
    a. results from injury to Broca's area.
    b. results from injury to Wernicke's area.
    c. is seen only when the visual cortex has been completely destroyed bilaterally.
    d. results from damage to the left visual cortex and the splenium (posterior part) of the corpus callosum.

18. Inability to follow instructions to move a limb in isolation results from
    a. disconnection of language areas from the pyramidal system.
    b. disconnection of language areas from the extrapyramidal system.
    c. damage to primary motor cortex.
    d. damage to Wernicke's area.

19. People with Williams syndrome
    a. have severe difficulties with even simple grammatical rules.
    b. have superior language abilities, but are retarded in nonlinguistic function.
    c. can draw beautifully, but cannot write.
    d. have almost total loss of Wernicke's area.

20. Dyslexic people
    a. are more likely than normal readers to have a bilaterally symmetrical cerebral cortex or to have language-related areas larger in the right hemisphere than in the left.
    b. are more likely to have small anatomical abnormalities, especially in the left frontal and temporal cortex.
    c. may have lateral masking by one letter of the immediately adjacent letters, but not masking of letters farther to the right.
    d. all of the above.

Answers to Multiple-Choice Questions

1. b	6. d	11. b	16. c
2. a	7. c	12. d	17. d
3. c	8. a	13. a	18. a
4. c	9. d	14. a	19. b
5. a	10. b	15. b	20. d

Diagram

Label the following areas related to language processing: arcuate fasciculus, Broca's area, face area of motor cortex, Wernicke's area, Sylvian or lateral fissure, visual cortex.

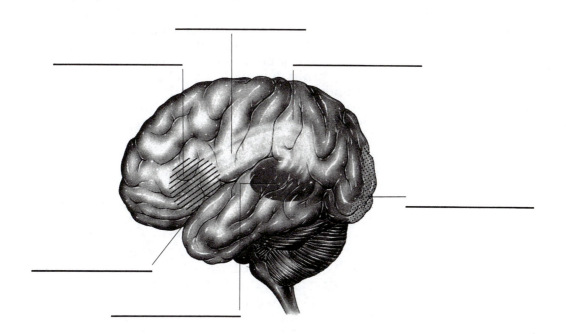

15

RECOVERY FROM BRAIN DAMAGE

INTRODUCTION

Brain damage can be caused by a variety of factors, including a sharp blow to the head; stroke; tumors; exposure to certain bacteria, viruses, or radiation; bullet wounds; and intake of drugs and toxic substances. Neuropsychologists can infer the location of brain damage by observing the type of behavioral deficits on tests such as the Halstead-Reitan test or the Luria-Nebraska neuropsychological battery.

Even after behavioral recovery from brain damage, the recovered behavior may be disrupted by stress or old age. Recovery may depend on a number of possible physiological mechanisms. Learned adjustments in behavior allow an individual to make better use of abilities unaffected by the damage and to improve abilities that were impaired by the damage, but not lost. Diaschisis, or decreased activity of neurons after loss of input, contributes to impairment following brain damage. It can be reduced by increasing neural activity through administration of stimulant drugs. Regrowth of axons can be promoted by Schwann cells, which provide both myelin sheaths,which serve as physical guides, and trophic factors. Sprouting of axons occurs in response to normal cell death, as well as after brain damage. Axons from undamaged neurons develop new terminals that attach to the vacant synapses. Sprouting can be facilitated by gangliosides, and may or may not be beneficial. Denervation supersensitivity refers to the increased sensitivity to a neurotransmitter of a postsynaptic cell that is deprived of synaptic input. It may explain why people can lose most of their dopamine-containing neurons in substantia nigra before exhibiting signs of Parkinson's disease. Reorganization of sensory representations can occur by activation of previously inactive synapses, denervation supersensitivity, or collateral sprouting.

Under some circumstances, damage to infant brains may be less debilitating than that which occurs to adult brains. This is because an infant's brain development can be modified so as to compensate for damage. Infant neurons have a greater capability for sprouting, and damage to one set of neurons may allow survival of other neurons that otherwise would have been lost. On the other hand, damage to an infant brain may be more disruptive than that to an adult brain, if it interferes with the organization of the brain.

The effects of brain damage may be less devastating if they occur in several stages (the serial-lesion effect), rather than in a single lesion of the same total size. Therapies for brain damage stress teaching people to take advantage of their unimpaired abilities. More recently, researchers have experimented with drug treatments, such as calcium channel blockers, and brain grafting. Because of the unique characteristics of fetal brains, fetal tissue is often used in such transplants. In some cases, the fetal tissue survives and extends dendrites and axons; in other cases, it may stimulate axon and dendrite growth by releasing trophic factors. Difficulties with use of fetal tissue for transplants include ethical concerns, a very brief period during development when the tissue is suitable, and the requirement for rapid transplantation after removal from the fetus. Patients receiving such transplants have received benefits, but have not been fully cured.

KEY TERMS AND CONCEPTS

Brain Damage and Mechanisms of Recovery
1. Causes of human brain damage
   Closed-head injury
   Stroke (cerebrovascular accident)
      Blood clot
      Rupture of artery
      Hypertension
      Causes of cell death
         Loss of oxygen
         Overstimulation
            Excessive calcium
            Activity at glutamate synapses
            Increased intracellular calcium, sodium, water
            Bursting of neurons
            Release of nitric oxide
      Means of lessening damage
         Magnesium
         Glutamate antagonists
         Reduction in body temperature
   Other causes: tumors, infections, drugs and toxins, bullet wounds, radiation, diseases

2. Diagnosis of brain damage
   Halstead-Reitan test
   Luria-Nebraska neuropsychological battery

3. The precarious nature of recovery from brain damage
   How stress impairs recovered behavior
      Cold or hypovolemia after lateral hypothalamus lesions
      Return of sensory neglect or sensory extinction
   Loss of recovered behavior in old age
      Loss of recovery from lateral hypothalamus lesions
      Parkinson's disease

303

4. Possible mechanisms of recovery from brain damage
    Learned adjustments in behavior
        Deafferented limbs
            One deafferented limb: lack of spontaneous use
            Two deafferented limbs: monkey learns to use both
    Diaschisis and its reduction
        Amphetamine
        Haloperidol
        Treatment of stroke patients
            Blocking norepinephrine synapses to control blood pressure
            Probable interference with behavioral recovery
    Regrowth of axons
        Myelin sheaths as guides
        Inhibiting growth of scar tissue: little effect
        Trophic factors from Schwann cells
    Sprouting
        Collateral sprouts
            Locus coeruleus
        Normal condition, not just response to damage
            Usefulness uncertain
        Gangliosides (glycolipids)
        Lesion of axons from cerebral cortex to hippocampus
            Innervation from opposite side of cortex
            Behavioral recovery correlated with electrical activity in
                hippocampus (reflecting collateral sprouting)
    Denervation supersensitivity
        Disuse supersensitivity
        6-OHDA (6-hydroxydopamine)
        Amphetamine: stimulation of intact side of brain
            Turning toward brain-injured side
        Apomorphine: stimulates supersensitive dopamine receptors
            Turning away from brain-injured side
        Parkinson's disease
            Symptoms only after loss of most dopamine-containing
                axons from substantia nigra
            Compensation by remaining axons
            Denervation supersensitivity
    Reorganization of sensory representations
        Activation of previously ineffective synapses
        Cortical reorganization
            Rapid for short distances (1 mm)
            Long-term reorganization for longer distances (10-14 mm)

Factors Influencing Recovery from Brain Damage
1. Age at the time of the damage
    Kennard principle

304

Altered connections by spared neurons
    Collateral sprouting
    Superior colliculus damage
    New connections not necessarily helpful
Effects on other, still developing neurons
    Removal of one hemisphere: increased thickness of other
        hemisphere
    Removal of anterior portion of cortex: less development of
        posterior cortex
    Early orbital frontal cortex damage: later developing areas
        compensate
    Early dorsolateral prefrontal cortex damage: effects more
        apparent later

2.   Differences between slow-onset and rapid-onset lesions
      Serial-lesion effect

3.   Therapies for brain damage
      Behavioral interventions
        Regain lost skills
        Use remaining abilities more effectively
      Drug therapies
        Nimodipine
            Calcium channel blocker
            Prevent damage due to excess NMDA stimulation
        Gangliosides
      Prospects for therapy by brain grafts
        6-OHDA
        Substantia nigra
        Fetal grafts
        Trophic factors
        Adrenal gland grafts
        Difficulties with fetal transplants for Parkinson's patients
            Tissue suitable only for brief period in development
            Transplant must be rapid
        Benefits, but not full cure

SHORT-ANSWER QUESTIONS

Brain Damage and Mechanisms of Recovery
1. *Causes of human brain damage*
   a. What is one source of damage in closed-head injuries?

   b. In what two ways does a stroke kill neurons? What are some treatments that may minimize damage?

2. *Diagnosis of brain damage*
   a. Describe two tests psychologists use to locate brain damage. Why does it take so long to arrive at an accurate conclusion?

3. *The precarious nature of recovery from brain damage*
   a. How do animals respond to cold and hypovolemia after recovery from lateral hypothalamic lesions?

b. What causes sensory neglect? What kinds of stimuli may cause
    a return to sensory neglect after recovery?

c. Why may deficits be uncovered by old age?

4. *Possible mechanisms of recovery from brain damage*
    a. List six potential mechanisms for recovery from brain damage.

b. How may learned adjustments in behavior be promoted?

c. What is diaschisis? How is recovery from diaschisis affected by
    amphetamine or haloperidol?

d. How may crushed, but not cut, axons in the peripheral nervous system form appropriate connections when they regenerate? What are two roles of Schwann cells in promoting regrowth?

e. With what neural connections is sprouting most likely to be useful? What evidence suggests that sprouting produces beneficial results?

f. What are gangliosides? How may they contribute to recovery?

g. What is denervation supersensitivity?

h. What are the effects of 6-OHDA? Explain the differential effects of amphetamine and apomorphine after 6-OHDA lesions.

i. What evidence is there that sensory representations may be reorganized during recovery? What was the surprise that investigators found when a monkey's limb had been deafferented 12 years earlier?

Factors Influencing Recovery from Brain Damage
1. *Age at the time of the damage*
   a. What is the Kennard principle? What evidence supports or refutes it?

   b. Discuss some ways an infant brain is better able to recover from brain damage.

   c. Under what circumstances is brain damage more disruptive to an infant brain than to an adult brain?

d. What are the differences in the time courses of recovery from early damage to the orbital frontal cortex and the dorsolateral prefrontal cortex?

2. *Differences between slow-onset and rapid-onset lesions*
   a. What is the serial-lesion effect? Through what means might it affect recovery from brain damage?

3. *Therapies for brain damage*
   a. What is a major emphasis of effective therapy for humans with brain damage?

   b. What are two potential drug therapies for brain damage? How may each work?

   c. What unique characteristic of the brain seems to make it amenable to tissue grafting?

d. Describe the experiment by Perlow and colleagues that used substantia nigra transplants.

e. What are two means by which transplants may promote behavioral recovery?

f. What are two possible sources of acceptable tissue for brain grafts? What are some difficulties associated with each?

POSTTEST

Multiple-Choice Questions

1. The most common cause of brain damage in young adults is
    a. stroke.
    b. disease.
    c. brain tumors.
    d. a sharp blow to the head.

2. Damage from strokes can be minimized by
    a. activating glutamate synapses.
    b. injecting magnesium to block entry of calcium into neurons.
    c. creating a fever.
    d. all of the above.

3. The Halstead-Reitan test
   a. takes about 8 hours to complete.
   b. contains a variety of measurements for numerous types of brain damage.
   c. includes many items, because a person may fail an item for a variety of reasons; results on one item must be compared with results on other items for an accurate diagnosis.
   d. all of the above.

4. Stress, cold, low blood glucose, hypovolemia, and aging
   a. can cause recovered rats to return to prerecovery behavioral deficits.
   b. do not affect recovered rats, although they cause normal rats to eat more.
   c. can cause recovered rats to become hyperactive.
   d. usually increase eating and drinking in rats with lateral hypothalamic damage.

5. Research on recovery from brain damage has shown that
   a. injections of transmitters can sometimes restore lost memories.
   b. a person has to completely relearn the skills and memories that were lost when brain cells were killed.
   c. the primary means of recovery is having some other area of the brain take over the function of the damaged area.
   d. recovery can sometimes occur when an individual is forced to make full use of remaining capabilities.

6. Amphetamine improves recovery by
   a. reducing diaschisis.
   b. increasing temperature.
   c. relieving stress.
   d. stimulating regrowth of axons.

7. Adequate regrowth of an axon does *not* occur when
   a. the axon is in the central nervous system of fish.
   b. an axon in the peripheral nervous system of mammals is crushed.
   c. the axon is in the central nervous system of mammals.
   d. all of the above.

8. Research on regrowth of axons in mammals has shown that
   a. inhibiting the formation of scar tissue is a highly successful new technique.
   b. Schwann cells release chemicals that inhibit growth of axons, in order to prevent the formation of cancers.
   c. neurons in the central nervous system may fail to regenerate because they lack trophic factors that promote this process.
   d. the reason that neurons in the central nervous system fail to regenerate is because there are no myelin sheaths there.

9. Sprouting
   a. occurs only in response to brain damage.
   b. is thought to be enhanced by gangliosides.
   c. is always maladaptive, since the wrong axons make connections.
   d. is enhanced by haloperidol.

10. Denervation supersensitivity is the result of
    a. increased sensitivity of nerve cells surrounding the one that has been damaged.
    b. neurons producing receptors for a different transmitter.
    c. changes in the chemical composition of the transmitter, making it more potent.
    d. an increased number of receptors on the postsynaptic cell or changes within the cell.

11. After 6-OHDA lesions were made on one side of a rat's brain
    a. amphetamine increased the release of dopamine mostly on the intact side and thereby caused the rat to turn in one direction (toward the damaged side).
    b. amphetamine directly stimulated postsynaptic receptors mostly on the intact side, causing the rat to turn in one direction.
    c. both amphetamine and apomorphine stimulated postsynaptic receptors on both sides of the brain, causing the animal to walk in a straight line.
    d. the primary means of recovery was collateral sprouting of neurons containing acetylcholine.

12. After amputation of one finger of an owl monkey
    a. neurons that had previously responded to it died because of lack of input.
    b. neurons that had previously responded to it became more responsive to other parts of the hand.
    c. reorganization caused the adjacent fingers to feel like the lost one.
    d. no reorganization could occur because connections become permanently fixed during the early critical period.

13. The Kennard principle
    a. states that infants have less ability than adults to recover from brain damage, since their brains are more fragile.
    b. is true only for the peripheral nervous system.
    c. is only partly correct, since children recover less well than adults from infection, poor nutrition, inadequate oxygen, or exposure to alcohol or other drugs.
    d. is only partly correct, since adults have greater ability to recover from destruction of a limited area of the brain.

14. Which of the following statements about recovery from damage in infant brains is *not* true?
    a. The main reason that infant brains *appear* to recover from damage more fully than adults is that they cannot be tested as thoroughly.
    b. Performance deficits may not be noticed for a year or more after damage to dorsolateral prefrontal cortex.
    c. During early development, damage to one set of neurons may alter the survival and connections of other neurons.
    d. Damage to infant brains can result in altered connections by the spared neurons.

15. The serial-lesion effect
    a. refers to the fact that after several consecutive lesions, animals recover behaviors in the same order in which they were lost.
    b. proposes that repeated brain damage is always more harmful than a single lesion of the same total size.
    c. opposes the parallel-lesion effect.
    d. refers to the fact that sometimes successive small lesions are less debilitating than a single lesion of the same total size.

16. Nimodipine
    a. is a type of ganglioside that can decrease the amount of damage caused by a stroke.
    b. is a calcium channel blocker that can decrease the amount of damage caused by a stroke.
    c. is a neurotoxin that destroys catecholamine neurons.
    d. is an immune suppressant that stops rejection of brain grafts.

17. Brain grafting
    a. would be more successful if there were no blood-brain barrier.
    b. succeeds only if the recipient of the graft is an infant or fetus.
    c. has been used with some success to promote recovery of adult rats with a rat version of Parkinson's disease.
    d. of the adrenal medulla has produced consistently excellent results in restoring function to Parkinson's patients.

Answers to Multiple-Choice Questions

1. d	6. a	11. a	16. b
2. b	7. c	12. b	17. c
3. d	8. c	13. c	
4. a	9. b	14. a	
5. d	10. d	15. d	

16

BIOLOGY OF MOOD DISORDERS, SCHIZOPHRENIA, AND AUTISM

INTRODUCTION

Depression is typified by fearfulness, gloom, unhappiness, helplessness, hopelessness, inactivity, and sleep disorders. It can occur as either a unipolar or a bipolar disorder. A unipolar disorder is one in which an individual displays only one extreme of mood. Bipolar disorder, or manic-depressive disorder, is characterized by cycles of depression and mania. During their manic phase, people are restless, uninhibited, excitable, impulsive, and apparently happy. Manic-depressive cycles may last a year or only a few days.

While the cause of depression is not fully understood, a number of possible factors have been identified. There may be a genetic component to depression and manic-depressive disorder, since they both tend to run in families. More recently, it has been suggested that depression may sometimes be caused by exposure to a virus at some point in life. Abnormal hemispheric dominance is sometimes associated with mood disorders; mania is associated with higher than normal activity, whereas depressed people have lower metabolic activity, especially in the left frontal lobe. Hormonal changes, such as during the premenstrual or postpartum periods, may trigger a depressive episode but are not the underlying cause of depression. Stress and allergic reactions can also trigger depressive episodes.

Drugs that improve affective disorders act in one of three ways: block reuptake of monoamines (tricyclics), inhibit monoamine oxidase (monoamine oxidase inhibitors, or MAOIs), block reuptake of only serotonin (fluoxetine). A major problem with the transmitter hypothesis is that drugs affect transmitter levels almost immediately but exert noticeable effects on mood only after two or three weeks. Alterations of sensitivity of either autoreceptors or postsynaptic receptors may underlie drug effectiveness; however, the mechanism of action is not understood.

In addition to treatment by drug therapy, mood disorders are sometimes treated with electroconvulsive therapy (ECT), sleep deprivation, bright lights, and lithium. ECT is particularly useful for patients who are unresponsive to antidepressants, who are suicidal and need immediate relief, or who suffer from delusions. Sleep- or REM-deprivation therapy is based on observations that depressed and manic-depressive persons enter REM sleep much sooner than normal persons and spend more than normal amounts of time in REM sleep. This may occur because their body temperature and activity cycles are out of phase. Exposure to bright lights is an effective treatment for seasonal affective disorder (SAD). Lithium is effective in treating manic-depressive disorder and if taken regularly, prevents relapse into either mania or depression. It may work by stabilizing dopamine and serotonin synapses.

Schizophrenia is an illness in which emotions are "split off" from the intellect. Its positive symptoms include hallucinations, delusions, and thought disorders. Negative symptoms include decreased or inappropriate emotional expression, decreased social interactions, and poor verbal communication. The brains of schizophrenics are lighter than those of normal people and have larger ventricles and fewer and more scattered neurons in the cerebral cortex and hippocampus, lower brain metabolism (especially in frontal areas), less task-induced metabolic activity, and poor lateralization of function.

Much evidence favors a genetic predisposition to schizophrenia. It is more common in biological relatives than in adopted relatives of schizophrenics and is more common in monozygotic than in dizygotic twins of schizophrenics. Also, adopted paternal half-siblings of schizophrenics, who did not share even the prenatal environment of the affected child, have a much greater frequency of schizophrenia than is found in the overall population. Genetics cannot completely explain the occurrence of schizophrenia, however, since the concordance rate for monozygotic twins is not 100 percent, and cases of schizophrenia do occur in families with no previous history of this disorder. Perhaps several genes on different chromosomes may predispose people to schizophrenia. One biological marker, which may predict schizophrenia independently of schizophrenic symptoms, is abnormal pursuit eye movements.

Stress does not seem to cause schizophrenia, although in some cases it may aggravate the symptoms. Another possible cause is a virus contracted in the prenatal environment. This hypothesis might explain the season-of-birth effect. It would also explain why some cases of schizophrenia occur in families with no history of the disorder. While conceptually appealing, there is not yet any direct evidence to support this hypothesis.

Symptoms of schizophrenia can be temporarily experienced by people who take large doses of drugs that stimulate dopamine synapses. However, drug-induced hallucinations are typically visual rather than auditory. Neuroleptic drugs, including phenothiazines (chlorpromazine: Thorazine) and butyrophenones (haloperidol: Haldol), block dopamine receptors. On the basis of such observations it has been hypothesized that schizophrenia occurs because of excess activity at dopamine synapses. There are a number of problems with this hypothesis. First, there is no consistent evidence of abnormally high levels of dopamine or its receptors in schizophrenics. Second, neuroleptic drugs decrease activity at dopamine synapses almost immediately but take two or three weeks to produce therapeutic benefits. An alternative to the dopamine hypothesis has proposed that schizophrenia might be caused by a deficit of glutamate activity due to increased inhibition by dopamine synapses.

The decision to administer neuroleptic drugs has been complicated by their potentially severe side effects. The most troublesome effect is tardive dyskinesia, which consists of tremors and other involuntary movements. This condition develops gradually and is more likely to occur in individuals for whom neuroleptic drugs are least effective. Unfortunately, the only way to decrease tardive dyskinesia is to increase the dose of neuroleptic, and the cycle continues. Recent advances in research have led to the use of new atypical antipsychotic drugs (clozapine, thioridazine), which appear to control schizophrenia without causing tardive dyskinesia. These drugs appear to control schizophrenia by affecting dopamine synapses in the mesolimbic system without affecting those in the basal ganglia, which contribute to movement. Clozapine also blocks serotonin receptors.

Autistic children are extremely withdrawn and exhibit a number of other symptoms, including stereotyped behaviors, resistance to change in routine, abnormal responses to sensory stimuli, insensitivity to pain, inappropriate emotional expressions, disturbances of movement, poor use of speech, and certain intellectual abnormalities. Some biological abnormalities such as abnormal patterns of metabolic activity, abnormal EEGs and irregular waking-sleeping cycles have also been observed in autistic children.

Autism is apparent at an early age and does not seem to arise from any lack of parental love. There is some support for a genetic basis of autism. It has been proposed that autism may occur when a large number of certain genes are present or when an individual has a fragile X chromosome. The latter hypothesis might explain why there is a lower rate of autism among girls; perhaps a second X chromosome might make up for problems with the faulty one. It has also been proposed that autism results from an overabundance of endorphins. At this time, there is little that can be done to help autistic children. Special education offers the most successful intervention.

Key Terms and Concepts

Depression
1. Types of depression
    Symptoms
        Fear and gloom
        Helplessness and hopelessness
        Inactivity
        Unhappiness
        Sleep disorders

Difficulties in diagnosing depression
    Persistence
    Interference with daily life
    Physical illness
Unipolar versus bipolar disorder
    Unipolar depression
    Manic-depressive disorder
        Mania
            Restlessness
            Excitement
            Laughter
            Mostly happy mood
            Rambling speech
            Loss of inhibitions
        Cycle length: days to a year

2. Possible biological causes of depression
    Genetics
        Little evidence for bipolar disorder gene on chromosome 11
        Probably several genes
    Viruses
        Borna disease
    Abnormalities of hemispheric dominance
        Mania: higher glucose metabolism
        Depression: lower metabolism, especially of left frontal lobe
        Damage to left hemisphere: depression
        Damage to right hemisphere: emotional unresponsiveness
    Events that trigger depressed eipsodes
        Hormonal changes
            Premenstrual depression
            Postpartum depression
        Allergic reactions
        Stressful events

3. Neurotransmitters and depression
    Antidepressant drugs and their effects
        Tricyclics
            Block reuptake of monoamines
            Imipramine (Tofranil)
            Side effects: dizziness, drowsiness, blurred vision, rapid
                heartbeat, dry mouth, excessive sweating
        Monoamine oxidase inhibitors (MAOIs)
            Decrease inactivation of monoamines
            Phenelzine (Nardil)

Second generation antidepressants
    Block reuptake of only serotonin
    Fluoxetine (Prozac)
    Fewer side effects than other antidepressants
    Occasionally provokes suicidal thoughts
    May alter personality
Implications for the physiology of depression
    Transmitter(s) involved
        Serotonin
        Norepinephrine
        Others?
    Problem of time course
        Antidepressant effects delayed 2 to 3 weeks
        Pharmacological changes within a few hours
        Increased transmitter in synapse
            Decreased autoreceptor sensitivity
        Decreased postsynaptic receptor responsiveness
    Complex mechanism

5. Other therapies for depression and bipolar disorder
Cognitive psychotherapy
Electroconvulsive therapy (ECT)
    Given with anesthetics or muscle relaxants
    Lower intensity than in early years
    Frequently given to right hemisphere only
    Used for patients who:
        Did not respond to drugs
        Are suicidal
        Suffer from delusions
    Occasional long-term memory loss
Alterations of sleep patterns
    Earlier REM sleep in depression or mania
        Correlated with body temperature
    Alter bedtime
    Sleep deprivation
    REM deprivation
Bright lights
    Seasonal affective disorder (SAD)
Lithium
    Bipolar disorder
    May have toxic side effects
    May stabilize receptors
    May lengthen circadian rhythms
    Blocks phosphoinositide

Schizophrenia and autism

1. Characteristics of schizophrenia
   Dementia praecox
   Not multiple personality
   Behavioral symptoms
       Positive symptoms
           Hallucinations
           Delusions
           Thought disorder
       Negative symptoms
           Decreased or inappropriate emotional expression
           Little social interaction
       Acute onset: greater probability of recovery
   Demographic data
       Approximately 0.7 percent of population: schizophrenia
       Approximately 1 percent of population: schizoid condition
       Reported 10-100 times more often in United States and Europe than in Third World
       More common in impoverished areas
       Diagnosed at earlier age in men

2. Brain atrophy or dysfunction
   Smaller brains
       Enlarged ventricles
   Fewer neurons in cerebral cortex, dorsomedial nucleus of thalamus, amygdala, and hippocampus
   Lower brain metabolism, especially in hippocampus and temporal and frontal cortex
   Less task-induced metabolic activity
   Disorganized neurons in hippocampus and cerebral cortex
   Poor lateralization of function

3. Possible causes of schizophrenia
   Genetics
       Twin studies
           Greater concordance for monozygotic than dizygotic twins
           Related to concordance for handedness
       Adopted children who become schizophrenic
           Paternal half-siblings
       Children of people with schizophrenia and their twins
       Search for schizophrenic genes
       Search for schizophrenic markers
           Saccadic eye movement
           Pursuit eye movement
       Beyond simple genetic determinism
           Schizotypy

Stress as a possible trigger
    May aggravate condition
    Probably not original cause
    Curt Richter's swimming rats
A virus?
    Season-of-birth effect
    Dorsolateral prefrontal cortex

4.   The biochemistry of schizophrenia
    Chemicals that can provoke a state similar to schizophrenia
        Amphetamine psychosis
            Large doses of amphetamine, methamphetamine, cocaine,
                LSD, or Antabuse
            Visual hallucinations
            Temporary
        L-DOPA
    Neuroleptics and the dopamine hypothesis of schizophrenia
        Phenothiazines
            Chlorpromazine (Thorazine)
        Butyrophenones
            Haloperidol (Haldol)
        Block dopamine receptors
    Strengths and weaknesses of dopamine hypothesis
        Strengths
            Effectiveness of dopamine-blocking drugs
            Increased eye blinking
        Weaknesses
            Dopamine levels not elevated at most times
                May be elevated for brief periods
            Dopamine receptors not consistently elevated
            Time course of effectiveness
        Possible answers
            Deficit of glutamate activity
    Side effects of neuroleptics and the search for improved drugs
        Neuroleptics decrease mesolimbic activity: beneficial effects
        Decrease activity of dopamine neurons that control
            movement: undesired effects
        Tardive dyskinesia
            Tremors and other involuntary movements
            No excess of dopamine receptors
            Permanent
        Atypical antipsychotic drugs
            Clozapine and thioridazine
            Greater blocking of mesolimbic dopamine receptors
            Clozapine: also blocks serotonin receptors

5. Infantile autism
   Symptoms
         Social isolation
         Stereotyped behaviors
         Resistance to change
         Abnormal responses to sensory stimuli
         Insensitivity to pain
         Inappropriate emotional expressions
         Disturbances of movement
         Poor use of speech
         Specific, limited intellectual abnormalities
   Biological abnormalities
         Regional differences of cerebral metabolic rate
         Deficient response to vestibular stimulation
         EEG abnormalities
         Irregular sleep-waking cycles
         Potentially hallucinogenic chemicals in blood
         Behave as if they feel cold
   Possible causes
         Not parental behavior
         Genetics
               High concordance in identical twins, not in other siblings
               Probably multiple genes
               Greater frequency in males
               Females: greater "dose" of abnormal genes to become
                     autistic
               Fragile X chromosome
         Endorphins
               Less response to painful stimuli
               Zeta receptor
               Children of drug addicts: some symptoms similar to autism
               High endorphin levels in some autistic children
   Therapies for autism
         Opiate-blocking drugs (naloxone or naltrexone)
         Special education

SHORT-ANSWER QUESTIONS

Depression
1. *Types of depression*
   a. Describe the symptoms of depression.

   b. What are some of the difficulties of diagnosing depression?

   c. What is the difference between unipolar and bipolar disorder? What is another term for bipolar disorder?

   d. Describe the symptoms of mania.

   e. What is the incidence in the population of unipolar depression? of bipolar disorder? What is the mean age of onset of each type of disorder?

2. *Possible biological causes of depression*
   a. What is the evidence for a genetic predisposition for mood disorders? Can it be concluded that depression is caused by certain genes on chromosome 11?

   b. What is Borna disease? What evidence links it to depression or manic-depressive disorder?

   c. Describe the evidence that depression may be related to abnormalities of hemispheric dominance.

   d. Damage or inactivity of which hemisphere may be associated with depression? with emotional unresponsiveness?

   e. What evidence suggests that hormones may affect depression? What is the likely relationship between hormones and depression?

3. *Monoamines and depression*
   a. Name three groups of antidepressant drugs and explain how each exerts its effects.

   b. Why is fluoxetine (Prozac) preferred over the monoamine oxidase inhibitors and the tricyclics?

   c. What are two controversies about fluoxetine's effects?

   d. Discuss the problems with the neurotransmitter hypothesis.

   e. What can we say about neurotransmitters and mood disorders?

4. *Other therapies for depression and bipolar disorder*
   a. How has electroconvulsive therapy been improved? For which three groups of patients is it most often used?

   b. What are the advantages and disadvantages of using ECT? What are some hypotheses about its mode of action?

   c. How do depressed individuals' body temperature cycles differ from those of nondepressed individuals? What sleeping abnormalities result?

   d. How might depressed individuals alter their sleeping schedules to alleviate their depression? How long do these results last?

   e. What is seasonal affective disorder (SAD)? How is it treated?

f.   What are the effects of lithium on manic-depressive disorder? How may it exert its effects?

Schizophrenia and autism
1.   *Characteristics of schizophrenia*
     a.   What is the origin of the term *schizophrenia*?

     b.   What are the positive and negative symptoms of schizophrenia?

     c.   What is the overall incidence of schizophrenia? Does this incidence vary among countries, economic levels, or sexes?

2.   *Brain atrophy or dysfunction*
     a.   What techniques have been used to study brain damage in schizophrenics?

b.   What brain abnormalities have been identified?

3.   *Possible causes of schizophrenia*
    a.   What evidence from twin studies suggests a genetic basis for schizophrenia?

    b.   What are concordance rates, and how are they used in studies of twins?

    c.   What evidence from adoption studies suggests a genetic basis for schizophrenia?

    d.   What advantage is there to studying paternal half-siblings?

e.   What is one biological marker for schizophrenia?

f.   What conclusions can be drawn about the role of genetics in schizophrenia?

g.   What is schizotypy?

h.   What role may stress play in schizophrenia?

i.   What is the season-of-birth effect for schizophrenia? How may this be related to a possible viral cause of schizophrenia? What are some unresolved problems with the viral hypothesis?

4. *The biochemistry of schizophrenia*
    a. What drugs can induce a state similar to schizophrenia? What
        are the similarities and differences between drug-induced
        psychosis and schizophrenia?

    b. What are two types of neuroleptic drugs?

    c. What is the evidence favoring the dopamine hypothesis of
        schizophrenia?

    d. What difficulties persist with this hypothesis?

    e. What other neurotransmitter has been hypothesized to be
        abnormal in schizophrenia? What is the relationship of this
        neurotransmitter to dopamine?

f. Neuroleptic drugs are thought to exert their beneficial effects on which dopamine system? Effects on which system are thought to underlie the unpleasant motor side effects?

g. What is tardive dyskinesia? In what type of patients is it most likely to occur? How is its treatment problematic?

h. What are two atypical antipsychotic drugs? Why are these drugs promising?

i. Why are they less likely than other neuroleptics to produce tardive dyskinesia? Receptors for which neurotransmitter, besides dopamine, are blocked by clozapine?

5. *Infantile autism*
    a. List the symptoms of autism

b.   What are some of the biological abnormalities in autism?

c.   Is parental "coldness" likely to be a factor in the cause of autism?

d.   What is the evidence favoring a genetic basis of autism?

e.   Why is autism unlikely to depend on a single gene?

f.   How might one explain the disproportionate number of autistic males?

g.   What is the fragile X syndrome? How may it be related to autism?

h.   What evidence suggests that autism may be based on excessive endorphin activity?

i.   What is the prognosis for autistic children? What type of therapy seems most beneficial?

POSTTEST

Multiple-Choice Questions

1. Which of the following is *not* a common symptom of depression?
    a.   excessive sleeping
    b.   fear and gloom
    c.   inactiveness or unproductive activity
    d.   unhappiness

2. Bipolar disorder
    a.   is characterized by cycles between depression and normal moods.
    b.   is characterized by cycles between depression and mania.
    c.   is more common than unipolar disorder.
    d.   is probably caused by excess activity in the mesolimbic dopamine system.

3. Which of the following is *not* true of depression?
   a. A gene on chromosome 11 is the cause of most cases of bipolar disorder.
   b. Hormonal changes before menstruation or after childbirth may aggravate a preexisting depressive condition.
   c. Serious undiagnosed physical disorders may cause or aggravate depression.
   d. It is likely that several different genes increase the risk of depression in different ways.

4. Research on Borna disease suggests that
   a. as in AIDS, a virus infiltrates the bloodstream and attacks the immune system.
   b. any illness that causes a fever also causes depression.
   c. a virus may cause depression or bipolar disorder.
   d. the viruses that affect animals cannot also affect humans.

5. During depression
   a. there is greater than normal activity in the left frontal lobe.
   b. there is lower than normal activity in the left frontal lobe.
   c. most people show symptoms of right-hemisphere damage.
   d. there is no indication of hemispheric imbalance, suggesting that environmental factors are the major determinant of depression.

6. Which of the following is *not* a type of antidepressant drug?
   a. monoamine oxidase inhibitors
   b. tricyclics
   c. serotonin reuptake inhibitors
   d. dopamine antagonists

7. Which of the following is true?
   a. The effects of drugs on transmitter systems are immediate, but their effects on depression are delayed for one to two weeks.
   b. The effects of drugs on transmitter systems are delayed for one to two weeks, but their effects on depression are immediate.
   c. Depression results from having too little of all the monoamine transmitters.
   d. The major effect of fluoxetine is to block serotonin receptors.

8. Autoreceptors
   a. when stimulated, increase the release of transmitter.
   b. are decreased in sensitivity by prolonged use of tricyclic drugs.
   c. are increased in sensitivity by prolonged use of tricyclic drugs.
   d. are blocked by most antidepressant drugs.

9. Electroconvulsive therapy
   a. is effective because it confuses patients and they forget their depressing thoughts.
   b. is rarely used anymore because of its bad reputation.
   c. is often used on patients who do not respond to antidepressant drugs or who are suicidal.
   d. is effective whether or not it induces a seizure.

10. Depressed people
    a. have their symptoms worsened by REM deprivation.
    b. enter REM sleep more slowly than do normal people.
    c. show an improvement lasting for many months after as little as one night's sleep deprivation.
    d. are sometimes helped by REM deprivation.

11. People with seasonal affective disorder (SAD)
    a. become more depressed during winter because of the cold.
    b. are frequently helped by sitting in hot sauna baths for an hour or more each day.
    c. are frequently helped by exposure to bright lights for 5-minute periods throughout the day.
    d. are frequently helped by exposure to bright lights for an hour or more before the sun rises or after it sets.

12. Lithium
    a. is helpful for depression but not for mania.
    b. is extremely safe because it is so simple.
    c. has many physiological effects, including stabilizing dopamine and serotonin receptors, lengthening circadian rhythms of temperature and sleep, and blocking synthesis of phosphoinositide.
    d. all of the above.

13. Schizophrenia
    a. refers to multiple personalities.
    b. refers to a split between the emotions and the intellect.
    c. is caused primarily by stress.
    d. is typically diagnosed in the elderly.

14. Which of the following is *not* a typical symptom of schizophrenia?
    a. visual hallucinations
    b. lack of social interactions
    c. delusions
    d. difficulty understanding abstract concepts

15. Studies of the brains of schizophrenics have revealed that
    a. they have fewer neurons in the cerebral cortex, dorsomedial nucleus of the thalamus, amygdala, and hippocampus.
    b. they have shrunken ventricles.
    c. they display abnormally high metabolic activity in the prefrontal lobe when they concentrate on tasks.
    d. they have abnormalities primarily in the parietal lobes.

16. Which of the following supports a genetic basis for schizophrenia?
    a. The season-of-birth effect is greater in families in which there is at least one schizophrenic relative.
    b. The concordance rate for schizophrenia is greater for dizygotic than for monozygotic twins.
    c. When twins are discordant for schizophrenia, the children of the nonschizophrenic twin are no more likely than the general population to become schizophrenic.
    d. Paternal half-siblings of schizophrenics are more frequently schizophrenic than would be predicted from the overall population frequency.

17. Research on possible causes of schizophrenia has demonstrated that
    a. conflicting messages from parents are a major cause of schizophrenia.
    b. abnormal pursuit eye movements may cause schizophrenia by providing unstable visual input.
    c. a prenatal viral infection may cause delayed symptoms at the time the dorsolateral prefrontal cortex should mature.
    d. the season-of-birth effect occurs more often in the tropics, where diseases are harder to control.

18. Drug-induced psychosis
    a. often lingers and causes a full-blown state of schizophrenia.
    b. is caused by drugs that increase the stimulation of dopamine receptors.
    c. is caused by drugs that block dopamine receptors.
    d. is characterized primarily by tactile hallucinations.

19. Which of the following is *not* an effective neuroleptic drug?
    a. haloperidol
    b. chlorpromazine
    c. clozapine
    d. L-DOPA

337

20. According to the dopamine hypothesis of schizophrenia, people with schizophrenia have
    a. excessive activity at dopamine synapses.
    b. deficient activity at dopamine synapses.
    c. glutamate in neurons that should release dopamine.
    d. too little dopamine activity in the mesolimbic system and too much in the basal ganglia.

21. Tardive dyskinesia
    a. gradually recedes once all traces of neuroleptic drugs have left the body.
    b. usually occurs soon after beginning neuroleptic drug treatment.
    c. is more likely to occur in older patients and those who have taken larger doses of neuroleptic drugs.
    d. develops because of increased numbers of dopamine receptors.

22. Overstimulation of mesolimbic dopamine synapses
    a. appears to cause tardive dyskinesia.
    b. may cause schizophrenic symptoms.
    c. produces visual hallucinations.
    d. causes excessive release of glutamate.

23. Atypical antipsychotic drugs
    a. include haloperidol and chlorpromazine.
    b. decrease dopamine activity primarily in the basal ganglia.
    c. decrease dopamine activity primarily in the mesolimbic system.
    d. should be avoided because they produce more tardive dyskinesia than do typical neuroleptics.

24. Symptoms of autism include
    a. increased sensitivity to pain.
    b. generalized mental retardation.
    c. complete lack of emotion.
    d. social isolation.

25. Which of the following is *not* true of autism?
    a. It usually results from lack of love in the family.
    b. Many autistic children have abnormal EEGs, irregular sleep-waking rhythms, attraction to heat sources, and deficient responses to vestibular sensation.
    c. A large number of autistic children have a fragile X chromosome.
    d. It may sometimes be related to high endorphin levels.

Answers to Multiple-Choice Questions

1. a	6. d	11. d	16. d	21. c
2. b	7. a	12. c	17. c	22. b
3. a	8. b	13. b	18. b	23. c
4. c	9. c	14. a	19. d	24. d
5. b	10. d	15. a	20. a	25. a